EDUCATION, DEMOCRACY AND POLITICAL DEVELOPMENT IN AFRICA

Education, Democracy and Political Development in Africa

Clive Harber

2 4 6 8 10 9 7 5 3 1

First published 1997 in Great Britain by
SUSSEX ACADEMIC PRESS
18 Chichester Place
Brighton BN2 1FF

and in the United States of America by
SUSSEX ACADEMIC PRESS
c/o International Specialized Book Services, Inc.
5804 N.E. Hassalo St.
Portland, Oregon 97213-3644

British Library Cataloguing in Publication Data
A CIP catalogue record for this book is available from the British Library.

Library of Congress Cataloging-in-Publication Data
Clive Harber
    Education, democracy, and political development in Africa / Clive Harber
        p.   cm.
    Includes bibliographic references and index.
    ISBN 1–898723–67–2 (hardcover : alk. paper). — ISBN 1–898723–68–0
(pbk. : alk. paper)
        1. Politics and education—Africa.   2. Education and state—Africa.
    3. Education—Political aspects—Africa.   4. Democracy—Africa.
    5. Education— Africa—Philosophy.   1. Title.
LC95.A2H37C   1997
379.6—dc21   97–20739
                                                                         CIP

Printed and bound by Biddles Ltd, King's Lynn and Guildford
This book is printed on acid-free paper

Contents

Preface and Acknowledgements

This book has its origins in an earlier work exploring the political nature of education in Africa (Harber, 1989). One theme of this book was the potential role of education in helping to shape democratic citizens. However, the bulk of the fieldwork for the book was carried out by 1987 and at the time there seemed little prospect that education for democracy would become a political priority in Africa. Most African countries were run either by single party or military regimes who regularly suppressed freedom of expression. An interest in the role of education in democratic development in Africa seemed somewhat perverse. However, as chapter 2 describes, from 1989 onward the pressures for democratic political change in Africa meant that such an interest was not so idiosyncratic. Indeed, as the case studies at the end of the book demonstrate, certain African countries have begun to include an overt commitment to education for democracy in their post-independence policy reforms.

The author and publishers gratefully acknowledge permission to use material previously published: chapter 5 is an amended version of an article that appeared in the *International Journal of Educational Development* 10(1): 27–36, 1990, courtesy of Elsevier Science Ltd, Kidlington, Oxford. Chapter 6 originally appeared in *Compare* 23(3): 289–300, 1993; I am grateful for the editor's permission to reprint it here.

In carrying out research on education for democracy in Africa I have been helped by many people and I would like to use this opportunity to thank them. However, certain individuals have been of exceptional assistance and should be mentioned here. In particular I would like to thank Peter Muyanda-Mutelu of the then African Social Studies Project in Kenya; Jonathan Lwehabura of the Ministry of Education in Tanzania; Tekeste Tesfamariam of the Ministry of Education and Zimmam Ghebrezghi of the Curriculum Development Institute in Eritrea; Patti Swarts and Roger Avenstrup of the National Institute for Educational Development in Namibia, and Rehabeam Auala and Nick Anim of the University of Namibia; John Pampallis of the Education

Policy Unit of the University of Natal; Ann Welgemoed of Grosvenor Girls High School, Durban; and Glenda Caine and Iole Matthews of the Independent Projects Trust in South Africa.

I have also benefited from discussions about education for democracy with many people but in particular I would also like to thank my wife Mary Harber, Lynn Davies and Audrey Osler of the University of Birmingham, Roland Meighan of the University of Nottingham, Bernard Trafford of Wolverhampton Grammar School, Veslemoy Wiese of the College of Telemark and all the education students that have participated in seminars held on the subject at the universities of Birmingham and Natal.

Clive Harber
University of Natal
Durban

1

Politics, Education and Democracy in the African Context

This book is concerned with the role played by education in helping to shape and sustain political systems in Africa. The book focuses primarily on formal education and its place in socialising young people into the political norms, values, attitudes and behaviours of democracy on the one hand and authoritarianism on the other. That there is a relationship between education and the nature of the political system was pointed out twenty-five centuries ago by the Greek philosopher Aristotle:

> But of all the safeguards that we hear spoken of as helping to maintain constitutional continuity the most important, but most neglected today, is education, that is educating citizens for the way of living that belongs to the constitution in each case. It is useless to have the most beneficial of rules of society fully agreed on by all who are members of the polity if individuals are not going to be trained and have their habits formed for that polity, that is to live democratically if the laws of society are democratic, oligarchically if they are oligarchic. (1962: 215–16).

This quotation underlines the key point that both democracy and authoritarianism are socially learned behaviours, they are not genetically inherited. However, this book is not as even-handed as Aristotle about the choice between oligarchy and democracy as it has a clear preference for the latter as a goal of political development because, though not necessarily easy to achieve, democracy provides the only political model which in the long run can provide the peaceful context for development that Africa so badly needs.

Chapters 2 and 3 of this book show how democracy has become clearly established as the preferred goal of political development in recent years and explore how this has affected both the nature of political debate in Africa and the potential role for education in helping to shape more democratic societies. However, the present contribution of education to democratic political development in Africa is problematic, despite regular lip-service to the rhetoric of 'educating democratic citizens' in the past. As chapter 4 suggests, formal education in Africa has historically been predominantly authoritarian in orientation though, as chapters 5, 6 and 7 illustrate, there have been attempts to challenge and change this at the levels of curriculum, school management and teacher education. One major obstacle to the success of such initiatives in Africa has been the political system itself which did not necessarily promote democracy or did so ambiguously and which did not systematically use the educational system to attempt to establish a more democratic political culture. This situation has now changed in certain countries and chapters 8, 9 and 10 examine three case studies – Namibia, Eritrea and South Africa – where education for democracy is now official policy as part of a process of wholesale political and educational transformation.

However, before exploring the relationship between education, democracy and political development in the African context in more detail, it is necessary to discuss some of the key concepts and ideas involved in the debate. The remainder of this chapter will therefore briefly discuss some important terms used regularly in the text.

Democracy and Authoritarianism

The term democracy comes from the Greek words *demos* (the people) and *kratos* (rule), thus meaning literally rule by the people. The size of population in most societies means that rule by the people in the sense of direct control of the state is impossible, so the formal structures of democracy include mechanisms to ensure a representative and accountable government which include, for example, a democratic constitution detailing the limits of each branch of government, regular fair and free elections, a choice of political parties, independence of the judiciary, the freedom to organise into pressure groups and a free and diverse mass media. In such a state political human rights such as freedom of speech, freedom of association, freedom of religion and freedom from arbitrary arrest are protected.

There is, however, a second aspect of democracy at the level of civil society, that is the need to create what Almond and Verba (1963) once called the 'civic culture', that is a political culture composed of values, attitudes and behaviours which are supportive of democracy at the level of the state. Democracy is about people actively participating in social and political institutions but it is important to note that democracy is not just about participating is also about how we participate. Participation rates were high in Nazi Germany and the

Soviet Union but this did not make them democracies. There are important procedural values underlying democracy which include tolerance of diversity, civility, peacefulness and mutual respect between individuals and groups. Other values include a respect for evidence in forming political opinions, a willingness to be open to the possibility of changing one's mind in the light of such evidence, the possession of a critical stance towards political information and a regard for all people as having equal social and political rights as human beings. In other words, in a democracy there should be an emphasis on reason, open-mindedness and fairness and the practice of moderation, cooperation, bargaining, compromise and accommodation.

Authoritarianism is the opposite of democracy. It is a political system where the government is not representative of the people and where the final power to remove a government is not in the hands of the voters as there are no genuine elections. There is no free political choice and the government is not accountable to the people for its actions. As the government is not accountable it is free to do what it wants and there are therefore no guaranteed human rights. Citizens have little say in how the country is run and rule is by edict and dictat. The one party and military regimes that have characterised post-independence Africa fall into this category as did the apartheid regime in South Africa.

Full information, regular discussion and tolerance of a range of viewpoints are not the characteristics of this type of culture. Diversity, critical thought and democratic participation are not encouraged or are actively suppressed. The leaders know they have the right answer and the role of the people is to obey and do what they are told to do. Those who do not obey the rules or who oppose the system are punished accordingly. Communication is top-down and hierarchical. The ideal citizen is one who is submissive, behaves according to the wishes of the regime, respects authority and does not ask any questions.

A key theme of this book is the need to reject authoritarianism and for education to contribute to the creation of a political culture of democracy which upholds values of tolerance and mutual respect. This involves upholding human rights and treating others as equal citizens regardless of, for example, ethnicity or gender. However, even in those states where considerable progress is being made in terms of education for democracy there are still serious issues to be faced and obstacles to overcome. Chapter 8 on Eritrea, for example, raises the issue of the treatment of Jehovah's Witnesses. Elsewhere sexual orientation is an issue. Chapter 9, for example, describes how Namibia has made considerable progress in the attempt to establish a democratic state and an education system that is supportive of democracy. Yet at the moment homosexuality would seem to be a blind spot. Whereas in South Africa discrimination on the basis of sexual orientation is forbidden under the constitution, in Namibia the President Sam Nujoma, has issued a two page statement to the effect that homosexuals should be 'uprooted'. He says:

> We are convinced that homosexuality is not a natural and objective form of moral history but a hideous deviation of decrepit and inhuman sordid behaviour. In reality lessons learned from the morals of our Namibian culture demonstrate that our morals are far more superior and acceptable to the vast majority of our people who adhered to Christianity . . . Homosexuality deserves a severe contempt and disdain from the Namibian people and should be totally uprooted. (*Mail and Guardian*, February 14–20 1997)

Whether or not one approves of homosexuality is not the issue. The issue is the fair and equal treatment of all human beings in a democracy. It is important when reading the last three chapters of the book to bear in mind that democracy and a human rights culture are still new and fragile in the three case study countries considered and that, as in other democracies, there many difficulties and contradictions even though progress has been made. It is also important for democrats everywhere to remember that democracy can always be both created and destroyed, both learned and unlearned.

Development

Originally the post-1945 discussion on development focused primarily on economic indicators such as national wealth, output and economic growth rates. Rich, industrialised countries were seen as 'developed' and poorer, predominantly agricultural countries were seen as 'developing'. However, social indicators of development such as literacy rates, school enrolment ratios and life expectancy have subsequently been added to attempts to measure levels of development in order to compare different countries.

All measures of development are controversial and problematic – the particular indicator used, for example, can change a country's international ranking quite significantly. Moreover, aggregate indicators are used for whole countries while there are rich in poor countries and poor in rich countries. However, broadly speaking and despite problems associated with particular indicators, African countries can largely be placed in the 'developing' category. Perhaps the most authoritative statement on this debate is the UNDP's annual *Human Development Report*. In its 1996 report, for example, 34 out of the 56 low-income (GNP $695 and below) countries were situated in sub-Saharan Africa. In terms of its general 'Human Development Index', which combines life expectancy at birth, adult literacy rate, school enrolment ratios and gross domestic product per capita, 37 out of 48 'low human development' countries were sub-Saharan (1996: 226–7). The remaining sub-Saharan African countries were placed in the middle categories respectively, none were in the high categories.

Most recently, and most relevant to this book, political indicators have been added to economic and social indicators in trying to assess development. Such indicators are essentially democratic in nature. The UNDP, for example, argues that 'The purpose of development is to enlarge all human choices, not just income' and one of its four essential components of the human development paradigm is empowerment: 'Development must be by people, not only for them. People must participate fully in the decisions and processes that shape their lives' (1995: 11, 12). While indicators such as human rights and political choice are not easy to measure, the UNDP has begun to discuss and evaluate political change in its assessment of world development trends. For example:

> Today, between two-thirds and three-quarters of the world's people live under relatively pluralistic and democratic regimes. In 1993 alone, elections were held in 43 countries – in some for the first time. The end of apartheid and the emergence of a free and independent South Africa in the 1990s marks a turning point for humanity. More than half of the African states are now undertaking democratic reforms and renewing civil society. (1995: 13)

Democracy and Civil Society

Diamond (1994) has argued that democratic consolidation in developing countries is facilitated by a pluralistic civil society that is composed of a wide range of organisations and associations. However, these groups must be both committed in their goals and methods to the deepening of the wider democratic process as well as other more particularistic group aims.

> In the wreckage left by predatory and weak, incompetent states, the mobilisation of civil society for democracy has perhaps been most striking in Africa. In a wide range of countries in sub-Saharan Africa – including Benin, Cameroon, Nigeria, Niger, Ghana, Kenya, South Africa, Zambia and Zimbabwe – and even such relentlessly unyielding dictatorships as Mobutu's in Zaire and Banda's in Malawi – the pressure for democratic change has been generated or advanced by autonomous organisations, media and networks in civil society. (1994: 58)

This can work both ways – the state deliberately encouraging and facilitating civil society in order to strengthen democracy or the growth of an associational civil society to counter a weak and ineffective state. In Mali in 1990, for example, Tuareg nomads took up arms against the then military regime accusing them of neglect and lack of development. In 1992 President Alpha Oumar Konare became Mali's first elected president following a popular uprising against the military government in 1991. Konare, like Nelson Mandela in South Africa, has consciously promoted dialogue and debate to heal the wounds of a divided society. The government have actively encouraged a civil society based on non-governmental organisations which were suppressed under the military, so that there are now some 3000 active local NGOs in operation as well as around 100 foreign ones (Lacville 1996). In Chad, on the other hand, where the notion of the state has become next to meaningless, there is now a network of several thousand local associations which practice a grass-roots form of democracy and have taken over some of the responsibilities of an ineffectual state. After thirty years of weak and undemocratic rule these are the best hope for the growth of a civil society that will in the long run eventually support and sustain a democratic political system (Tuquoi, 1996).

If groups organise themselves democratically with a proper constitution, representation, elections, transparency and accountability, they can help to habituate significant parts of a society towards democratic norms and practices through their members' experiences. However, given that such norms and practices are learned rather than genetic, if the formal education system itself is also geared towards education for democracy then the wider population will share such values and both a democratic civil society and a democratic state will be correspondingly stronger.

Ethnicity

Ethnic groups tend to be defined by a unity of language, culture and religion often based on occupation of common territory at some time in the group's history. Ethnicity has often been regarded as a destabilising factor in post-independence African politics because primary identification with, and loyalty to, the ethnic group has weakened the state and the ethnic 'winner takes all' approach to elections and the subsequent distributions of the spoils of office have weakened democratic processes in particular. However, while discussion of ethnicity is unavoidable in the context of African politics, it must be remembered that ethnicity is not necessarily a rigid and fixed social phenomenon but is fluid and complex with the construction of ethnicity depending on the particular context in question. While some groups have existed for a long period of time and were incorporated into the new states during the colonial period and at independence, others are of much more recent creation and are often defined by outsiders or in relation to the state. An example would be the Kalenjin of Kenya which in reality is a collection of smaller groups that are of increased significance in contemporary Kenya because the President, Daniel Arap Moi, is a Kalenjin and there are conflicts and controversies surrounding accusations of favouritism in the allocation of state resources.

Before colonialism, ethnic groups in Africa were not so clearly defined. However, colonialism began a process of enhancing the importance of ethnic identity by its use in relation to birth certificates and identity cards. Some colonial regimes also exaggerated or invented traditional ethnic rivalries with 'divide and rule' policies as was the case in Zimbabwe, Namibia and even more dramatically in South Africa. Ethnic conflict increased in the period leading up to independence as nationalist politicians widened the scope of ethnic identity to gain a larger basis of support so that the power of the state could be used to reward the areas that supported them with roads, hospitals and schools. Post-independence politics has seen a perpetuation and deepening of this trend towards ethnic political conflict over resources. Bayart's book *The State in Africa* has the interesting sub-title 'The Politics of the Belly'. He puts it thus:

> in Africa ethnicity is almost never absent from politics, yet at the same time it does not provide its basic fabric . . . in the context of the contemporary state ethnicity exists mainly as an agent of accumulation, both of wealth and political power. Tribalism is thus perceived less as a political force in itself than as a channel through which competition for the acquisition of wealth, power or status is expressed. There are many examples of this. The tensions between the Igbo and non-Igbo in Port Harcourt and between Yoruba and Hausa in Ibadan, reveal not so much disembodied linguistic or cultural oppositions as a struggle for the control of the town and its resources in the first case, or for the trade in kola and cattle in the second. (1993: 55)

Ethnicity and ethnic competition are important in African politics and are unlikely to disappear. However, creating a political culture more supportive of democracy means changing the rules of ethnic engagement to promote greater dialogue, tolerance, respect and compromise between ethnic groups. In particular it means working towards a rejection of violence as a means of solving political disputes. Education can play a part in the development of these values.

The Political Nature of Schooling

Formal education is not a neutral or technical exercise. It is intimately bound up with values, competing goals and with such questions as education for what? – what sort of citizen and what sort of society are we trying to create through education? One writer on Tanzania, for example, notes that:

> There are books and articles in learned journals which discuss at length the role of education in development. Some treat the subject as if it were above politics and propaganda. Tanzania subscribes to the notion that there is no such thing as value-free education. (Mmari, 1979: 120)

The content of education in Africa expressed in terms of curriculum, syllabuses and textbooks has, for example, tended to reflect the dominant ideologies and policy concerns of governments. During the colonial period this was expressed in terms of the superiority of the European imperial culture and the inferiority of African cultures. Colonialism was portrayed as generously bringing the benefits of civilisation to end tyranny and chaos. In the post-colonial period the messages changed but the influence of a dominant ideology remained. In Kenya, for example, textbooks have tended to reproduce capitalist values concerned with achievement, the work ethic and becoming 'modern'. In Tanzania,on the other hand, syllabuses have had a clearly socialist tone while in Nigeria, given the historical experience of civil war based on ethnicity, there is an overwhelming priority given to issues of national unity and nation building. In South Africa before 1994, and the then Rhodesia, school textbooks reflected the racist forms of government in power. In post-independence Zimbabwe, on the other hand, school history textbooks took on a distinctly Marxist tone. Elsewhere dominant ideologies have been closely linked to particular leaders. In Zaire the ideology of 'Mobutuism' has been still used as a mechanism of politically controlling education and students as was Nkrumahism in Ghana (Harber, 1989).

Essentially during this period schools have been largely involved in a process of political indoctrination or political socialisation, that is thay have often been teaching values and beliefs as though they were truths or facts to be absorbed. The process may well have involved deliberately falsifying or ignoring counter viewpoints or evidence as well as presenting information in a biased way to achieve a desired end. In this way the aim is that students will learn preferences and predispositions to certain values even though they may be aware that other viewpoints are available. As will be discussed in more detail in chapter 4, this has been facilitated by whole school and classroom organisation which is authoritarian in nature and hence which discourages participation, questioning and independent thought.

However, while authoritarianism has characterised mass formal education a small minority have attended elite schools. While also authoritarian, a key purpose of these schools is to train the few to lead the many and thus to inculcate expectations of leadership through the ethos, location, physical structure, curriculum and routines of the school. Chapter 10 on South Africa describes Michaelhouse as an example of such a school. Another example is Kamuzu Academy in Malawi which was founded by then President of Malawi, Dr Hastings Kamuzu Banda in 1981. Entrance to the school is highly competitive. In 1986, for example, 20,000 children took the entry test but only 90 were accepted (Allen-Mills, 1987). The school is closely modelled on the British public school and its geographical remoteness combined with its covered walkways, arches, sweeping lawns, expansive playing fields and lake explain its nickname of 'Eton in the bush'. Classics (the study of the ancient Greek and Latin languages) is a compulsory part of the curriculum. All instruction is in English. Students heard speaking Chichewa are liable to be punished. The school was deliberately and explicitly created for the minority that Banda hoped would go on to become the leaders of Malawi.

Democratic Education

Democratic education differs significantly from authoritarian schooling. It does not begin with a set of existing answers to be learned and repeated. There is no 'successful' outcome in terms of the nature of the opinions held by students. It stresses the ability to make up one's own mind after consideration and discussion of relevant evidence. It is therefore 'learner-centred' and based on the procedural values outlined in the section on democracy above. This has certain implications for both whole school organisation and classroom method.

If students are going to learn both the skills of participation and to value toleration, mutual respect and equality then they must experience them in practice rather than just learn about them in an abstract way. In a democratic school students are involved in the nature and organisation of their own learning and such a school will therefore involve some shift of power and authority away from staff and to students. In a democratic school students will, for example, be expected to be involved in some way in school management, usually through a mechanism such as some form of elected school council with at least some powers over matters of significance to students and on which their views are represented along with teachers and parents. It will also mean more opportunity for student control of what they learn in the curriculum. Here there is a long continuum of possible levels of freedom of choice – from the complete freedom that has existed at certain private schools in the United Kingdom and America, to subject options and courses in which students are allowed some self-direction through negotiated study and project work.

In terms of classrooms this means greater variety in teaching methods with students participating and being actively engaged in learning on a regular basis. Discussions, group work, projects, visits, simulations and independent study will all be used more frequently than in a traditional, authoritarian school. Also, a more diverse range of assessment techniques will be used in addition to examinations based on memorisation. This might include, for example, assignments and course work, individual and group projects, orals and skill-based exercises where students are asked to show comprehension and analysis of evidence rather than simply learn material off by heart and repeat it.

However, it is important to stress that democratic education implies genuine variety in learning styles, not the complete replacement of authoritarian methods with constant participatory ones. Young people need to experience many different forms of learning and interaction if they are to develop as flexible, balanced and self-sufficient individuals. At certain times this means being able to digest and organise information provided by others quickly, at other times it means knowing how to look for information oneself; it also means knowing how to discuss in order to clarify thinking about a controversial issue or having the skills to argue a case convincingly. The need for flexibility means that students must be regularly exposed to a variety of teaching and learning contexts. In the traditional authoritarian school currently predominant in Africa this is not possible as the emphasis is overwhelmingly on teacher-dominated transmission. On the other hand, more democratic and participant forms of school and classroom organisation which are characterised by greater negotiation and consultation allow for students to experience a wide range of teaching and learning possibilities including, ironically, teacher-led contributions.

A more flexible and varied education is a more suitable preparation for democratic citizenship than a move from teacher-centred authoritarianism to an over-emphasis on continual group work. This is because, as Almond and Verba (1963) argued in their classic book on the 'civic culture', democracy requires a mixture of active and passive behaviours and capabilities in its citizens. It needs individuals with the abilities to participate actively and to learn independently but also to sit and listen quietly to teachers and other students and to obey rules agreed to by a majority.

School Effectiveness and Peace

One of the themes that occurs in this book is the notion of school effectiveness – in particular that a democratic school is more effective than an authoritarian one. School effectiveness, as with education in general, can only really be considered in relation to goals – effective at what? The goals and purposes of education are inevitably both diverse and controversial because they are based on values – what different people believe are the most important outcomes of schooling. While there is considerable evidence that more democratically organised schools are more effective in terms of the conventional goals of schooling such as examination results (Davies and Harber, 1997; Dimmock, 1995), this book assumes that peace should be an essential goal of education in the African context.

During the last thirty years Africa has been plagued by wars which have wreaked havoc on economies and seriously damaged the social fabric of many countries. During the 1980s, for example, the war in Mozambique caused the destruction or closure of 60 per cent of the country's schools (World University Service 1994). Education in the context of violent civil conflict is a major theme of the final three chapters of this book on Eritrea, Namibia and South Africa. Authoritarianism has been an important cause of this violence. Authoritarian regimes in Africa have been marked by violent suppression of human rights, violent resistance, civil unrest and wars against neighbours. While democracies are far from perfect, accountable and representative government minimises internal violence and the abuse of human rights, and greatly decreases the possibility of going to war without good reason. The development of a democratic political culture and civil society encourages the spread of values supportive of the non-violent resolution of political conflict. Education for democracy is therefore an education for peace and is of fundamental importance in judging school effectiveness in Africa. As the Director-General of UNESCO has put it:

> Wars will not cease, either on the ground or in people's minds, unless each and every one of us resolutely embarks on the struggle against intolerance and violence by attacking the evil at its roots. Education

offers us the means to do this. It also holds the key to development, to receptiveness to others, to population control and to the preservation of the environment. Education is what will enable us to move from a culture of war, which unhappily we know only too well, to a culture of peace, whose benefits we are only just beginning to sense. (Tedesco, 1994: 1)

Conclusion

The themes outlined in this chapter are the major themes of this book and are discussed in more detail in the chapters that follow. As will already be clear, this is not a neutral book. Politically the book supports democracy as the model of political development for Africa and rejects authoritarianism. It believes that in the future people in Africa should enjoy basic political human rights and freedoms and live in a context where emphasis is placed on the peaceful settlement of disputes. It also argues that education has the potential to play an important part in the gradual creation of democratic societies and states in Africa. However, simply providing more education of the traditional authoritarian type will not help. As educational aims, priorities and outcomes are ultimately based on values, formal schooling is always an ideologically contested terrain. This book sides with those in Africa who want to see schools become less autocratic, less violent, more participatory and more open institutions. This will be a long, slow struggle and may never be fully achieved but, as the following discussion demonstrates, at least the debate is finally on the agenda.

2

Political Change in Africa

A strong, united and democratic Africa that rests on the genuine happiness and the freely given consent of the majority is the one best placed to contribute meaningfully to world peace and stability. (Kenyan novelist Ngugi wa Thiongo, 1992)

If we in the AFPRC don't want to hold elections in the next thousand years, then there will be no elections. (Captain Yahya Jammeh, Chairman of the Armed Forces Provisional Revolutionary Council, Gambia quoted in *Focus on Africa*, January–March 1996)

In the late 1950s and early 1960s, when most of the new states of sub-Saharan Africa gained their independence from colonial rule, there was considerable optimism about the development of democracy. Yet by the early 1970s most African states were ruled either by one-party or military regimes. Moreover, neither the ex-Portuguese colonies of Angola, Mozambique and Guinea-Bissau which became independent in the mid 1970s nor Zimbabwe, which became independent in 1980, looked like following a path of multi-party democracy.

Yet since the late 1980s there has been a renewed interest in democracy in Africa. In Zambia Kenneth Kaunda became the first ever African Head of State to lose his position through competitive, democratic elections. There have also been democratic, multi party elections in, for example, Kenya, Ghana, Angola, Benin, Cameroon, Ivory Coast, Mali, Niger, Lesotho, Malawi and South Africa – all previously authoritarian regimes.

The three most recently independent countries in Africa – Namibia, Eritrea and South Africa – have all adopted a democratic political system. Between 1990 and 1994, 41 out of 47 countries in sub-Saharan Africa underwent some measure of political liberalisation, even though only 14 countries have so far achieved a political transition to a minimally 'democratic' regime while others have experienced transitions which are flawed or blocked (Bratton, 1994: 1). Democracy, however, is certainly on the agenda again in Africa. This chapter discusses both the factors which have hindered African democracy in the past and those which have led to the renewed interest in democracy.

Democracy and Authoritarianism in Africa

Historically, while many pre-colonial African societies established certain checks and balances to oversee rulers, monitor their actions and call them to account, the predominant pattern was more authoritarian with highly personalised rule, faith in the wisdom and justice of rulers rather than belief in laws and procedures, unequal rights of citizenship and the absence of formal opposition (Chazan, 1993: 71). One Kenyan writer, for example, has argued that whereas many African scholars and politicians have portrayed African societies before colonialism as harmonious and enjoying democratic tranquilities,

> what comes out of a careful examination and analysis of the political institutions and mechanisms of the pre-colonial African societies is a mixture of the rudiments of democratic tendencies and practices on the one hand and aristocratic, autocratic and/or militaristic tendencies, with varying degrees of despotism on the other . . . However, colonialism unleashed such violence, discrimination and exploitation that Africans, young and old, educated and uneducated, soon forgot the violence and undemocratic practices of their traditional rulers. (Simuyu, 1988: 51–2)

As Simuyu suggests, the tendency, with some exceptions, was for traditional authoritarian systems to be replaced by colonial authoritarian systems where colonial governors enjoyed wide powers with very few restrictions and dealt with opponents by jailing them, as many of the future leaders of Africa experienced for themselves. The period of transition between colonial rule and democratic elections and independence was usually a very short one allowing little time for democratic practices and values to become embedded either in society or in political leadership. Moreover, the nationalist reaction to colonialism was itself not particularly democratic:

> The decision to dismantle the colonial apparatus was the culmination of the call for liberation. But the by-products of democracy seen in terms of freedom were far more uncertain. Emphasis was put on consensus as opposed to tolerance, on loyalty in contrast to self expression, on identity and not on individual rights, on political boundaries but hardly on procedures. Nationalism in many parts of Africa was not, in any fundamental sense, liberal. (Chazan, 1993: 75)

Democratic institutions in the newly-independent states faced serious obstacles: ethnic divisions and a shallow sense of nationhood, fragile political institutions and political leaderships only weakly committed to democracy, limited managerial and technical talent, high popular expectations in severely restricted economic circumstances and a tendency, in the absence of a vigorous private sector, for political leaders to see the state as the prime source of personal enrichment. In some countries, such as Angola and Mozambique, the new governments were faced with armed rebel movements. The new states were therefore very fragile and potentially unstable and this fragility often led in an undemocratic direction for, as Mazrui has noted, 'the African state is sometimes excessively authoritarian to disguise the fact that it is inadequately authoritative' (1983: 293). More recently, for example, the repressive and racist nature of the white minority regime in the then Rhodesia, the violent and conspiratorial nature of the liberation struggle and the resulting prominence of Marxist-Leninism in post-colonial Zimbabwe have helped to produce tendencies towards intolerance, distrust and violence in the political culture (Sithole,1988). Indeed, a cartoon in a South African newspaper gave the following definition of democracy according to 'The Robert Mugabe Dictionary': 'government by stacking the decks against opposition parties, incitement of fear and homophobia, media restrictions, harassment of opponents etc.' (*The Mercury* 20 March 1996).

Post-colonial authoritarianism in Africa has been characterised by:

> the removal of constitutional rights and protection from political opponents, the elimination of institutional checks and balances, and the centralisation and concentration of power in presidential offices, as well as the termination of open party politics and the regulation and confinement of political participation – usually within the framework of a single ruling party. (Jackson and Roseberg, 1982: 23–4)

The movement to one-party and subsequently military rule was publicly justified and defended on a number of grounds including the waste of scarce resources involved in party competition, the tradition of a single unchallenged chief and the idea that a single mass party could represent everybody anyway without resorting to parties based on narrow ethnic support. Indeed, it became fashionable to argue that authoritarian regimes provided the necessary discipline for development in Africa. This 'developmental dictatorship' argument, as Sklar (1986) has called it, reasoned that the suppression of human rights and freedoms was justifiable if this led to economic growth, more education, better housing and a higher standard of living. One writer noted that when he became seriously interested in Africa nearly twenty years ago, 'The picture I was given was that Africa did not want or need democracy and, anyway, was incapable of making it work' (Wiseman, 1990: ix).

Yet the picture is not as uniformly bleak for democracy as these general historical trends suggest. First, in Nigeria, for example, as in many other countries, there has been strong popular support for the idea of democracy and choice of leaders, even though the corrupt and ethnically biased practices of politicians, institutions and the public themselves may leave much to be desired (Wiseman, 1990: x; Harber, 1989: 89; Peil, 1976: 45). Second, there are strong forms of cultural resistance to authoritarianism. Chazan, for example, refers to the resilience of the democratic ethos in Ghana in the face of virtually continuous abuse and corruption by civilian and military elites:

> A deeply ingrained indigenous culture of consultation, autonomy, participation and supervision of authority . . . has enabled Ghanaians to combat the uncertainties of state domination and the tyranny of its leaders. Lawyers, students, unions and traders have also evolved a culture of resistance to interference in their affairs. (1988: 121)

Third, some countries, such as Botswana, have successfully retained democratic political structures. This has been facilitated in Botswana by certain cultural and political factors. The Tswana groups that go to make up Botswana share similar languages and cultural traditions and the ruling party has gone out of its way to treat all ethnic groups equally. The ruling party has also built on the tradition of the 'kgotla', a village communal assembly used to consult public opinion and gain local public support for policies prior to implementation. Moreover, the emphases in Tswana traditional culture on moderation, non-violence and obedience to the law as well as public discussion and community consensus have also facilitated and helped to sustain democratic government' (Holm, 1988).

The New Pressure for Democracy Inside Africa

The West African journalist Cameron Duodu (1992) wrote:

> The West must accept that the wish for democracy in Africa is genuine. Very often one hears westerners murmuring that perhaps Africans 'have their own way' of doing things and democracy does not 'quite suit' them. That is not only balderdash but downright racist. If Africans can fly complex jet fighters or carry out intricate research into genes, why can't their leaders be made to understand freedom of expression and freedom from arbitrary arrest?

The context for the recent movement back towards democracy in Africa has been the collapse of communism in eastern Europe. Not only did this undermine the Marxist-Leninist model of development chosen by countries such as Ethiopia, Mozambique and Zimbabwe but also meant that western governments stopped seeing African regimes in cold-war terms. It was no longer justifiable to support dictatorships simply because they were anti-communist and pro-western. A prime example of the result of these cold-war policies in Africa is Somalia where for twenty-three years the repressive dictator Siad Barre stayed in power by using the country's strategic geographical position to get aid by playing the Americans off against the Russians (Huband, 1992).

General Obasanjo, a former Nigerian Head of State, as chair of a conference of the African Leadership Forum in April 1990, has commented:

> The changes taking place in eastern Europe have far-reaching political implications for the Third World in general and for Africa in particular. The winds that swept away dictatorships and autocratic one-party systems and state structures, inefficient economic systems and unresponsive social institutions in eastern Europe, and fueled a democratic rejuvenation and the observance of human rights, are not unfamiliar in Africa. The winds of change in eastern Europe are providing considerable opportunities for the African people and oppressed peoples the world over to intensify their struggle for democracy. (quoted in Kpundeh, 1992: 1)

Within Africa a number of factors have fuelled this debate. Opposition by African governments to apartheid in terms of the principle of one person, one vote began, with the end of apartheid clearly in sight, to look somewhat contradictory when other Africans are denied the same right in their own countries. At the same time Africans have become increasingly self-critical.

After thirty years of independence the previous tendency to explain the poor economic, social and human rights record solely in terms of the colonial experience and subsequent neo-colonial relationships began to look partly like shifting the blame. Moreover, authoritarian regimes have clearly not delivered the development promised. Indeed, it has recently been argued that the evidence globally suggests that democracy is more conducive to long term economic growth than authoritarianism. While a number of South-East Asian economies (South Korea, Taiwan and Hong Kong) have developed rapidly this is despite being ruled by authoritarian government rather than because of it. Indeed, if authoritarianism were the deciding factor then Africa would be an economic giant which it clearly is not (*The Economist*, 27 August, 1994). Vernon Mwaanga, the foreign minister of Zambia, has noted that, while African governments do not deserve all the blame, the one-party or military system has monopolised the process of finding solutions and as a consequence 'Our best brains have fled Africa for America or Britain because when they came up with honest opinions they were called dissidents and hounded out' (Rawnsley, 1990).

As a result of such factors there has been a marked increase in agitation for democratic political reform inside African countries from the late 1980s onwards. The movements pressing for such reform have been primarily urban and have represented a coalition of groups such as students, trade unionists, intellectuals, lawyers and teachers. The church has also played an important role in drawing attention to the abuse of human rights as have dissident politicians and former bureaucrats who have become disenchanted with authoritarian regimes because of their repressive nature and their failure to manage the economy successfully (Healey and Robinson, 1992: 129–30). Consequently the case for democratisation has become increasingly recognised at official levels. A conference held in Arusha, Tanzania in February 1990 was attended by over 500 delegations representing grass-roots organisations, non-governmental organisations, United Nations agencies and governments. 'The African Charter for Popular Participation in Development and Transformation', which was adopted by the plenary, holds that the absence of democracy is a principal reason for the persistent development challenge facing Africa,

> We affirm that nations cannot be built without the popular support and full participation of the people, nor can the economic crisis be resolved and the human and economic conditions improved without the full and effective contribution, creativity, and popular enthusiasm of the vast majority of the people. After all, it is to the people that the very benefits of development should and must accrue. We are convinced that neither can Africa's perpetual economic crisis be overcome, nor can a bright future for Africa and its people see the light of day unless the structures, pattern, and political context of the process of socio-economic development are appropriately altered. (Kpundeh, 1992: 34)

However, if the newly-formed democratic political institutions are to survive in the long term and beyond the first round of elections then they will need to be grounded in a more supportive political culture. The values of a political culture are not inherited genetically but must be learned socially and formal education must therefore play an important part in this. One book on democracy in Africa noted that:

> Finally, without exhausting the list of possible useful changes, one may note the need for civic education to develop a more tolerant political culture, a deeper commitment to and understanding of political institutions, and a more mutually trustful political climate. (Diamond, 1988a: 28–9)

The importance attached to education is reflected in the views of Africans. One Kenyan writer, for example, argues forcefully that:

> the amount or degree of democracy in any given society is directly

proportional to the degree of acculturation of the people in democratic values, attitudes and beliefs. For democracy to exist, survive
and prosper, it requires that the people be bathed in and drenched
with the democratic ethos! It is in this manner that education and
culture constitute one of the most fundamental foundations of democracy . . . education must preach the gospel of equality, freedom and
human dignity. (Gitonga, 1988: 22)

At a series of workshops organised by the US Agency for International Development held in Benin, Ethiopia and Namibia and
involving scholars, government officials, journalists, lawyers and
political activists from over forty African countries, the participants
stressed the importance of education. They noted, for example, that
political education for democracy was important because 'individual
ignorance of personal rights and understanding of what democracy
means has encouraged authoritarianism in Africa'. It was suggested
that student councils in schools could help to teach students about
real ideas and practices in democratic management. There was also
clear agreement among participants in the three workshops that some
form of resocialisation towards a democratic political culture was
necessary as 'negative values had been inculcated for so long'.
One participant in the Ethiopia workshop stated that 'if we are
to recognise that our societies are heterogeneous, maybe we can
overcome the fear of transition with a culture of tolerance . . . How
to reach it? Through mutual recognition, consensus, compromise, not
fear'. Another participant added that education would be crucial to
the development of a culture of tolerance which, it was hoped, would
contribute immensely to the creation of an enabling environment for
democracy: 'We must encourage citizens to learn the habits of civil
disobedience on a massive scale . . . We must encourage people to go
out and demonstrate, to show their opinion regarding issues, because
we must eliminate the culture of fear' (Kpundeh, 1992: 24–5).

As Vernon Mwaanga, the foreign minister of Zambia, put it:

Of course, democracy is going to be painful for Africa. Very painful.
There is a huge job of education to be done. We have to learn the arts of
persuasion, not fighting. But show me an alternative which isn't worse.
Our trouble with democracy is that we've never tried it. (Rawnsley,
1990)

External Pressures

Outside of Africa the end of the cold war has witnessed a growing
consensus both internationally and among western governments in
particular on the need actively to promote democratic government.

This consensus is summed up in the words of the United Nations itself, which is now clear that political freedom and democracy are an essential ingredient of human development:

> The purpose of human development is to increase people's range of choices. If they are not free to make these choices, the entire process becomes a mockery. So, freedom is more than an idealistic goal – it is a vital component of human development. People who are politically free can take part in planning and decision-making. And they can ensure that society is organised through consensus and consultation rather than dictated by an autocratic elite. (UNDP, 1992: 26)

In order to promote democracy political conditions are now attached to almost all western aid to Africa whether from individual governments or from institutions like the World Bank. The holding of a multi-party election in Kenya in 1992, for example, was directly influenced by the suspension of western aid. USAID (1993a) makes the position of the American government very clear:

> People throughout the world have demonstrated by their own actions that freedom is a universal concept. Men and women have risked their lives for the proposition that liberty, dignity and individual worth are not just the province of those living in the developed world. The influence of democratic ideas has never been greater . . . Because of the menace generated by non-democratic regimes and because democracy and respect for human rights coincide with fundamental American values, the Clinton Administration has identified democracy promotion as a primary objective of US foreign policy. Foreign assistance is a natural vehicle for achieving this goal. In accordance with Administration policy and congressional mandate, USAID will decline to provide any form of assistance, except to meet humanitarian needs, to governments that engage in a consistent pattern of gross violations of internationally recognised human rights. Further, when allocating scarce development resources among countries, USAID will consider a government's human rights performance, including its willingness to permit the emergence and functioning of democratic institutions and independent political groups.

The British Overseas Development Administration (ODA) uses the expression 'good government' in describing the conditions it attaches to aid. Good government is defined as one which is legitimate in that it is based on the consent of the governed and can be removed by them; accountable in that there are checks and balances to the power of government, a free media and transparency in decision-making; competent in that it can formulate appropriate policies, make timely decisions and implement them effectively; and is also a government that respects human rights and the rule of law. The ODA notes that:

> Bilateral aid has always been conditional but is now more overtly conditional on good government criteria. Conditionality means withholding, or threatening to withhold, aid unless or until conditions

set by the donor are met. Aid is also increasingly used positively to encourage governments who have embarked upon change in this area . . . Aid conditional on good government criteria has a role to play in encouraging democracy through transparency and accountability of government. (British Council, 1993: 3)

The Danish development agency DANIDA has adopted a similar policy:

human rights and democracy have now come to occupy a central place in Denmark's development cooperation effort. This is true both at the policy level, where these issues are pursued in the policy dialogue with different countries, and increasingly at the operational level too. (DANIDA, 1993: 7)

DANIDA notes that the approach of engaging in dialogue with the authorities has borne fruit in a number of countries and useful practical agreements have emerged on Danish assistance for initiatives to promote respect for human rights, democratic development and better government. These countries have included Uganda, Burkina Faso, Ghana, Mozambique, Ethiopia and Benin. On the other hand, it proved impossible to engage in similar meaningful dialogue with Malawi, Kenya and Sudan and as a consequence development co-operation has been scaled down or discontinued (DANIDA, 1993: 8–9).

A similar emphasis on aid being tied to progress towards democratic government can be found in the publications of other western aid agencies as is suggested simply by glancing at their titles – *Support for Democratic Development* (Royal Norwegian Ministry of Foreign Affairs, 1993); *Development Cooperation and Processes Towards Democracy* (Finnish International Development Agency, 1991) and *Rights, Democratisation, Governance and Development* (Canadian International Development Agency, 1993).

However, as the experience of DANIDA suggests, the efforts of international agencies in promoting democracy in Africa have not always been successful and western agencies have not necessarily been consistent in withdrawing aid in support of democracy. Bratton (1994) describes the Western commitment to democratisation as half-hearted. Factors such as continuing close ties with former colonies, enduring cold-war alignments, the giving of greater emphasis to economic liberalisation and the importance of oil have all meant that the West has not been as insistent about tying aid to democracy as it might have been and the resulting transitions to democracy have been problematic. In Nigeria, for example, the military government ignored the results of a general election held in 1993 and have continued in power despite a lengthy pro-democracy strike by oil workers. In Kenya, President Daniel Arap Moi, despite agreeing to an election in 1992 after international pressure, has gradually resorted again to authoritarian tactics since aid has been restored. The Nairobi *Daily Nation* commented:

> Are we alone in experiencing the chilling feeling that Kenya is regressing towards the authoritarianism of the not-so-recent past? Yesterday's newspapers carried reports of two more opposition MPs and a newsman being arrested, with several similar cases pending; anti-government legislators complain repeatedly of being harassed, prevented from opening offices . . . (13 April 1994)

Indeed, Kenya's main aid donors called an unscheduled meeting for July 1995 because they feared that the country was backing away from democratisation. Germany was especially critical with a member of the German embassy in Nairobi saying that 'Kenya tries to do a bit of window-dressing before each donors meeting only to reverse everything as soon as aid has been pledged' (*The Guardian*, 4 May 1995). This still did not stop state-sponsored violence against members of the opposition Safina Party later in the year (Tunbridge, 1996).

However, it is important that when such aid and loan conditions are imposed by the West and support the broad principles of democracy they should not provide detailed blueprints as Africans must design their own approach to democracy in their own contexts. Detailed interference in the internal democratic politics of a country is unacceptable. Recently, for example, President Joaquim Chissano of Mozambique complained that he was under pressure from foreign governments to agree to a power-sharing deal in advance of elections:

> There are some people saying that even those who lose the elections should govern along with those who win. There are pressures and influences . . . This is a model that is being recommended very insistently and with a certain imposition. (*The Guardian*, 11 July 1994)

Western governments and aid agencies not only seem, in principle at least, to favour democratisation of African political systems, they also see education playing an important part in the process. However, they are not yet completely clear about the role education could or should play in this regard. Thus, DANIDA, for example, notes that, 'Education, information and training in human rights are central to long-term development prospects and essential if respect for human rights is to be upheld and sustained' (1993: 16) while the Norwegian government argues that:

> For the growth and consolidation of a democratic system, it is important that the attitudes and values of such a system, like respect for human rights, should be expressed and reflected in different contexts. For example, in the educational system information about democracy and human rights needs to be imparted from the elementary

level onwards. (Royal Norwegian Ministry of Foreign Affairs, 1993: 19)

However, neither document explains in more detail how education might contribute. Yet, as the rest of this book will suggest, the education needed to support democratisation must be about more than the provision of information called for in the two above quotations. It must be not only education *about* democracy but also *for* democracy, in the sense of developing political skills, and *in* democracy in the sense of developing values by providing experience of democracy at the school and classroom level. The British ODA recognise this in their recent education policy paper in a section called 'promoting good government':

> The relationship between education and the political process is highlighted in the recent ODA Technical Note on Good Government. The relationship is illustrated in Eastern Europe and the former Soviet Union where the process of democratisation is seen to be hampered by curricula based on authoritarian philosophies and characterised by rote learning. Citizens who have been exposed to learning styles which require the questioning of assumptions, empirical styles of study, and the exploration of alternatives, are seen as likely to have more chance of participating fruitfully in a pluralistic political process than those who have not. There is some evidence that political instability declines not only as income rises but also as education improves and that political freedoms and civil liberties tend to be associated with progress in education. (ODA, 1994: 3)

While the rest of the document does not develop this statement in terms of policy guidelines, the British Council, which works very closely with the ODA, held a seminar to develop such guidelines in 1994 and USAID held a similar seminar in late 1993. Political conditionalities to aid for education in Africa and elsewhere may therefore not be long in coming.

However, if such political conditionalities are to be realised then some attention will have to be paid by Western governments to the insufficient public resources now going into education. It is much more difficult to educate for democracy if there are very large classes, insufficient textbooks, too many unqualified teachers and pupils are dropping out of school because parents cannot afford fees. Indeed, the very same governments and institutions that now promote democratisation in Africa have been responsible for a deterioration in the quality of education over the last ten years. In a study of the effects of structural adjustment programmes on education in Africa and Latin America, Reimers (1994: 128) concludes that:

> In sum, adjustment either directly via the effects on education or indirectly via the incentives facing households, reduced educational opportunity. But it reduced it particularly for the disadvantaged . . . If

we assess the impact of adjustment programmes on education with the standards proposed earlier, that is in terms of whether countries that adjusted are doing better than those that are not, it is clear that adjustment has fallen short of these targets.

If schools and classrooms are to be altered to encourage democratic values it will cost money. While it is to be hoped that renewed economic growth in African countries will help to pay for some of the required improvements in education, the 'developed' industrialised countries have a responsibility to contribute to the resources required for democratisation. This would mean, for example, cancelling debt burdens, paying more positive attention to the social sectors in structural adjustment programmes and meeting the the UN agreed target for aid to developing countries of 0.7 per cent of gross domestic product.

Rather than the traditional World Bank and structural adjustment programme emphases on 'cost-saving' and 'efficiency' in education, the problem needs to be looked at in another way. How 'efficient' is it if education cannot afford to educate for democracy? This point is made, for example, by Stephen Heyneman who is an American senior education official with the World Bank. He has written of a change of opinion stemming form his experience in Eastern Europe, though the point he makes is also relevant to Africa:

> Wherever I have worked over the last decade I have recommended the use of educational vouchers and other measures to maximise user choice. But after working on the educational problems of Central and Eastern Europe and the Russian Federation, I have changed my opinion. My view has changed not because educational efficiency is no longer important. Rather, it has changed because I have discovered that the importance of educational efficiency has a limit. In the case of Russia I have been working with an ethnically heterogeneous, federal system, much like our own but falling apart. More than 100 ethnic groups now may control schools and, not having the traditional restraints may now be able – if they choose – to teach disrespect for the rights of their neighbours. Schools can contribute to armageddon, and I have been forced to learn that there are things in life – such as civil unrest and civil war – which are more expensive than an inefficient and cumbersome public education system. But let me begin at the beginning. What is there that makes an education system essential for a consensus of democratic values and for the creation of a democratic society? (Heyneman, 1995: 1)

Conclusion

In Africa at the present time neither authoritarianism nor democracy is fully institutionalised. However, debates and pressures in the future will undoubtedly be concerned with the rate of progress towards democracy and the obstacles in its path. Education is now widely recognised both inside and outside Africa as having a potentially important role to play in this process of political development. Explaining and conceptualising the nature of political development and the role of education in it is the role of theory. Yet, as the next chapter will argue, education in the past has been seen in the literature on political development theory as contributing more to the possession of 'modern' bureaucratic attitudes and behaviours than to democratic ones. Before going on to look at the nature of education in Africa in more detail, it is therefore important first to re-examine interpretations of political development in the context of debates about democratisation and what type of education is most congruent with democratic politics.

3

Turning Full Circle: Education, Democracy and Political Development Theory

This chapter examines the relationship between education, democracy and political development. It does so in the first instance primarily in the light of one of the two major schools of thought about political development – modernisation theory. Dependency theory, the other major school of thought, is less helpful to this discussion because it is more concerned with existing neo-colonial relationships between developed and underdeveloped countries rather than with ultimate goals of development. As one book on national development has put it:

> Perhaps the most serious difficulty with dependency theory has been its failure to provide a viable strategy for development . . . the important question is what kind of dependency and what kind of development should be pursued in any given context. The dependency theorists have given very few guidelines in this regard. (Fagerlind and Saha, 1989: 25)

Modernisation theory, on the other hand, is centrally concerned with questions of destination – what does a 'modern' individual or society look like and how does a country change from 'traditional' to modern? Political modernisation theory has been primarily concerned with the nature of the 'modern' state and civil society. Particularly influential in determining the nature of this debate was a group of American political scientists writing in the 1960s who were members of, or associated with, the Social Science Research Council's Committee on Comparative Politics. The publications of these writers have set the agenda of debates about political development of the last thirty years. Higgott (1983: 17) has usefully classified this work into three categories:

1   Theoretically oriented case studies of individual countries such as

      those of Apter (1957) on Ghana, Coleman (1958) on Nigeria and
      Pye (1962) on Burma.
2   The Princeton University Press volumes of the Comparative Com-
      mittee on Political Development (La Palombara, 1963; Pye, 1963;
      Ward and Rustow, 1964; Coleman, 1965; Pye and Verba, 1965; La
      Palombara and Weiner, 1966; and Binder et al. 1971).
3   The more generally theoretical volumes in the Little Brown series,
      the most important of which were Almond and Verba (1963),
      Almond and Powell (1966) and Pye (1966).

The work of this group of political scientists will be discussed in
the next section. The first focus of this discussion will on the place
of democracy within political modernisation. A second focus will be
on the role of formal education in political modernisation and its
potential contribution to democratic development. This second theme
will necessitate further consideration of liberation theory which was
a theory of the role of education in development that was initially
associated with dependency theory but which now needs reconsid-
eration in the light of its potential contribution to debates surrounding
democratisation.

Democracy as Modernisation

One of the major problems of political modernisation theory is the
confusion of 'is' and 'ought' questions. Sometimes writers argue for
a particular form of development as one that ought to be aimed for
while others base their theory around matters as they presently are
and project this into the future. These two ways of looking at political
modernisation have influenced thinking about democracy and political
development.

O'Brien (1972) shows clearly how early writers on political development showed a strong commitment to representative democracy
as a political goal. A key figure in this emphasis on democracy was
the American political scientist Gabriel Almond who chaired the
SSRC from 1954 to 1963. In his writing there is a clear preference
for democracy as the ultimate goal of development. He notes, for
example, that the 'voyage towards democracy and welfare' will be
'long and uncertain' but he has little doubt that the ship will reach port
(Almond and Powell, 1966: 338). While genuinely democratic political
processes cannot be achieved in the immediate future 'in the new and
modernising nations of Asia, Africa and Latin America, the processes
of enlightenment and democratization will have their inevitable way'

(Almond, 1970: 232). However, others were just as hopeful. David Apter, for example, held it as 'an article of faith' that in the new states 'the long term prognosis for democracy is hopeful' (1965: 38).

A corollary of this aim of democratic development was the emphasis give to the importance of political culture and political socialisation. Political culture is the pattern of values and attitudes about politics held by a population and is shaped by the history, geography and socio-economic structure of a society whilst it, in turn, influences the way in which a society's political institutions operate. Such attitudes may, for example, include those towards how political change should take place, those towards deviation, dissent and disagreement and feelings towards major offices and national symbols. Political socialisation is the process whereby these values and attitudes are learned from various agencies such as the family, the school and the mass media. For writers such as Almond, therefore, key questions were the nature of the political culture that was most supportive of democracy and how this might be developed where it did not already exist.

In the second half of the 1960s, however, the earlier optimistic emphasis on democracy gave way to a new, more pessimistic emphasis on stability and order. In part this reflected the changing nature of the membership of the SSRC committee on comparative politics. Lucien Pye was appointed to the chair of the committee in 1963 and Samuel Huntington and Aristide Zolberg went on to the board in 1967. Pye, and to a lesser extent Huntington, were important theoreticians of counter-insurgency and Huntington and Zolberg both wrote books on political order in the new states. In conjunction with this was the evidently unstable nature of politics in the developing world and the conspicuous weakness of post-colonial political institutions leading to a pattern of civil war and military coups d'état. To talk of democratic development in such circumstances seemed increasingly far-fetched. As O'Brien saw it in the early 1970s:

> The great majority of recent American scholarship is agreed on one basic point, that few hopeful prospects can be held out to most of the underdeveloped world in the absence of the creation of new and more effective political institutions . . . the new institutional order should be the work of political elites, able and willing to impose new structures on the masses from above. The ideal of 'democracy', of effective popular representation in the process of government, is in this perspective in the short run not merely irrelevant but in effect positively dangerous. (1972: 362)

Moreover, from the perspective of the United States government, embroiled in an escalating war in Vietnam, order and stability were of greater significance than democracy for in disorder and instability the then communist arch enemy could thrive. Better a pro-American authoritarian regime than the risk of an unstable democratic one. The close links between American universities and government departments and the official advisory role of many political scientists also therefore also helped to bring about a declining academic emphasis on the desirability of democratic politics in America's client states in the developing world. Linked to this was an increasing concern over law and order in the United States itself in the wake of the dissent and violence associated with the civil rights and anti-Vietnam war movements and even, from Samuel Huntington in particular, a resulting admiration for the seemingly orderly political life of the then totalitarian Soviet Union. Indeed, a recent analysis of Huntington's significant contribution to modernization theory has argued that:

> Throughout his work there runs a strong current of dislike for the confusing, disturbing and contradictory aspirations of the masses, and an admiration for any 'elite', bureaucracy or 'leadership' capable of containing, chanelling and if necessary suppressing them. (Leys, 1996: 67)

The last theoretical volume of the SSRC Committee on Comparative Politics series was entitled *Crises and Sequences in Political Development* (Binder et al., 1971) and this effectively represented the collective thinking of the committee. Political development was seen as a political system's capacity to cope with five crises: legitimacy, identity, participation, penetration and distribution. Governmental capacity referred specifically to governing elites and crises were therefore seen from the perspective of threats to the position of those elites and the necessity of elites for the maintenance of order. As one commentator has noted, 'the interest in order of those at the top is given a logical precedence over the interest in social justice of those below' (Sandbrook, 1976: 180–1).

Finally, Higgott (1983: 26–36) identifies an extension of this trend in political science in the development of public policy analysis in relation to developing countries in the 1970s and early 1980s. This is a rational choice, problem-solving, managerial approach to providing technocratic solutions to political problems. The emphasis is on the output side of the political system and systems maintenance, and it again gives priority to the role of elites in a highly centralised bureaucratic state and in this sense differs very little from the order-based modernisation theory of the late 1960s.

Education and Political Development

By the end of the 1960s and early 1970s, therefore, modernisation

theory emphasised order over democracy and stability over representation and accountability, even if this meant regimes whose human
rights records left much to be desired. This change in emphasis is
paralleled in modernisation theory's discussion of education. In *The
Civic Culture* Almond and Verba (1963) investigated the question of
which type of political culture best supported a democratic political
system and the extent to which certain political socialisation agencies, including education, contributed to the development of these
values. Political cultures were differentiated according to the degree
of participation with a 'civic culture' containing a high proportion
of citizens who take an active role not only in terms of voting but
also in terms of having high levels of political interest, knowledge,
opinion formation and organisational activity. Linked to this was the
idea that citizens in a civic culture would have a high level of political
efficacy – both the competence to participate and the belief that
political participation can change policy. Education was found to be
a key factor supporting the development of this ability to participate.

However, despite this emphasis on the importance of participation
in a democracy, the study unfortunately sheds little light on the
equally important question of *how* citizens participate in a democracy.
As Almond and Verba state:

> the orientations that distinguish the educated from the relatively
> uneducated tend . . . to be affectively neutral . . . The educated indi-
> vidual is, in a sense, available for political participation. Education, how-
> ever, does not determine the content of that participation. (1963: 382)

Rather than use the opportunity to redress the situation by discussing the important question of the nature of participation in a
democracy, a subsequent SSRC-sponsored book specifically on education and political development (Coleman, 1965) neatly sidestepped
the question in the manner of the second-wave of order-oriented modernisation theorists and defined a modern state as neither necessarily
democratic nor non-democratic. Coleman quotes the above finding
from Almond and Verba and states that it 'is consonant with our
working definition of political development, which we deliberately
sought to make affectively neutral, that is, not loaded in favour of
either a democratic or a non-democratic direction'. For Coleman a
modern state is a participatory state but this can be either participation
in the forced, centrally directed and monolithic fashion of an authoritarian state or equally by free and voluntary association in a democratic
state (1965: 15, 20). As a result education is seen as contributing to a
modern, participatory state essentially through the mass development
of bureaucratic skills: 'Formal education has a cardinal role to play

in producing the bureaucratic, managerial, technical, and professional cadres required for modernisation.' Moreover, literacy not only makes a modern communications system possible but also helps to develop rational-secular attitudes and allows for effective government 'penetration', i.e. the population will be sufficiently literate to understand what the government is telling them to do (Coleman, 1965: 17).

While Almond and Verba and Coleman's books were concerned with what constituted the modern polity and how education contributed to it, the work of Alex Inkeles (1969a, b, 1974) focused much more on individual modernity – what does a 'modern' individual look like and which socialisation agencies most contribute to individual modernity? While his findings point to education as the major determinant of a modern person, like Coleman and also in the manner of the second wave of modernisation theorists, Inkeles attempts to adopt a 'neutral' definition of political modernisation:

> In the case of politics, the temptation was great to define as modern those qualities presumably characterising the participants in a democratic polity. To do this, however, was to open ourselves to the charge of of being culture-bound, a stigma which students of comparative systems wish to avoid at all costs . . . we can hardly insist that the qualities which most characterise the democratic man are necessarily the best, certainly not those which exclusively suit one for life in the political structure of a modern society, at least as long as we acknowledge the modernity of Russia and (pre-Second World War) Japan and Germany . . . If we could discover such common requirements (of citizenship) to exist despite the enormous differences in the formal structure of these political systems, we surely would be entitled to speak of those qualities that are truly appropriate to the modern as opposed to the democratic citizen. (1969a: 1121–2)

For Inkeles, the modern citizen is one who takes an active interest in public affairs, is informed about important events and decisions and participates in civic affairs. However, most importantly the citizen must understand the ways in which bureaucratic rule and impersonal criteria of judgement replace treatment based mainly on special personal qualities, on family ties or friendship and connections, for the modern polity is 'suffused with bureaucratic rationality' (1969a: 1122). He acknowledges that this definition is similar to that of Almond and Verba's analysis of the participant qualities required of citizens in a democratic civic culture but, unlike Almond and Verba, argues that it applies equally to citizens in a totalitarian state such as the then Soviet Union. For Inkeles, and as argued above, the key distinction between authoritarianism and democracy lies not in a proclivity to participation but in how participation takes place:

> The difference between what is expected of a citizen in a democracy

as against an extremist or totalitarian regime lies not in the qualities designated above but along different dimensions. I have elsewhere described the non-democratic syndrome as containing exaggerated faith in powerful leaders and insistence on absolute obedience to them; hatred of outsiders and deviates; excessive projection of guilt and hostility; suspicion and distrust of others; dogmatism and rigidity. Any, indeed all, of these qualities which are common in the non-democratic personality could quite easily be combined with any or all of the qualities which Almond and Verba defined as characteristics of the democratic citizen. (1969a: 1123)

In his empirical research (Inkeles and Smith, 1974: ch. 9) Inkeles found education to have the strongest relationship of all variables with the possession of modern (i.e. bureaucratic) attitudes, values and behaviour as described above. The explanation for this is the congruence between the bureaucratic nature of 'modernity' and the bureaucratic nature of school organisation. For example, the pupil at school learns new skills such as reading, writing and arithmetic so that he or she will later be able to 'read directions and instructions and to follow events in the newspaper' and this produces a heightened sense of personal efficacy. Most revealing of all, however, is the way in which pupils learn impersonal rules from the hidden curriculum of school organisation:

> School starts and stops at fixed times each day. Within the school day there generally is a regular sequence for ordering activities: singing, reading, writing, drawing, all have their scheduled and usually invariant times. Teachers generally work according to this plan, a pattern they are rather rigorously taught at normal school. The pupils may have no direct knowledge of the plan, but its influence palpably pervades the course of their work through school day and school year. Thus, principles directly embedded in the daily routine of the school teach the value of planning ahead and the importance of maintaining a regular schedule. (Inkeles and Smith, 1974: 141)

For modernisation theory, therefore, the school contributes to the development of the modern state and the modern individual by providing the requisite bureaucratic skills, values and behaviours rather than democratic ones. As O'Brien argued in his analysis of modernisation theory cited above:

> Democracy as an effective modern political ideal appears to rest ultimately on some form of institutionalised tension between bureaucracy and popular influence in government: a balance between authority and liberty . . . the argument of this paper is that the balance in America over the past decade has been increasingly weighted on the side of authority, hierarchy and bureaucratic order. Political scientists in their writings reflect this change. (1972: 351–2)

The Return of Democracy and Political Culture

In recent years, as Gabriel Almond (1993) has himself noted, the wheel seems to have turned full cycle and there has been something of 'a return to political culture' in political science. Part of this has been the beginnings of a renewed interest in the question of the relationship between political culture and democracy, particularly in relation to political development. This renewed interest in political culture has undoubtedly been influenced by the new global consensus on the desirability of democratic political development that has followed the collapse of communism in eastern Europe, which is discussed in chapter 2 in relation to Africa. However, as Diamond (1993) points out, until very recently political scientists have been more interested in the nature of elite political culture needed to re-establish democracy rather than the mass political culture necessary to sustain it. He notes that:

> Perhaps it is no coincidence that concern with the development of a mass democratic culture, as an important factor in the emergence and consolidation of democracy, has been most evident recently in the writing of democratic citizen activists directly engaged in the tasks of civic education and mobilisation. Perhaps they have grasped something that the main currents of academic political science have missed in the past two decades: that political culture does matter to democracy, independently of other variables, and that the development of a democratic culture *cannot be taken for granted as a natural by-product of democratic practice or institutional design.* (1993: 7 – italics added)

We seem to have returned thirty years later to the early years of modernisation theory where democracy is the acknowledged goal of political development and the key questions are what sort of political values and attitudes best support and facilitate democratic political systems and how are such values best transmitted to the population? At the individual level the question can be rephrased in terms of what sort of values should a democratic person possess and how are these values best learned?

In terms of the question of values it is important to think not only in terms of political knowledge and skills of participation as modernisation theorists have tended to do but rather also in terms of the key question raised earlier – how should citizens participate? A useful start here is to simply reverse the list of authoritarian characteristics provided by Inkeles and described above so that the ideal democratic citizen would possess the following characteristics: flexibility, trust, efficacy, a critical open-mindedness, tolerance of other viewpoints and mutual respect for the persons holding them, a belief in the equality of all people as human beings, a respect for evidence in forming opinions and, as Inkeles nicely puts it, an attitude towards authority that is neither 'blindly submissive' nor 'hostilely rejecting' but rather 'responsible . . . even though always watchful' (quoted in Diamond, 1993: 12).

Such values indeed cannot be taken for granted and, at the mass level, education must therefore play an important part in their creation and consolidation.

Liberation Theory Reconsidered

One school of thought about political development, liberation theory, has been particularly influential in making the case for a connection between education and political development. Liberation theory is not a complete or systematic theory of development in the same way as modernisation or dependency theory though, as in the latter case, it does owe its origin to a Marxist perspective. Liberation theory is built on the assumption that as a result of colonial and neo-colonial relationships there are both oppressors and oppressed in underdeveloped societies. The oppressors are either the colonial power or the rich neo-colonial power-holders who succeed them after independence and who both share the values of the former colonialists and need to perpetuate inequality, injustice and authoritarianism in order to serve their own interests and protect their privileges. The oppressed, on the other hand, are the poor, often illiterate peasants and workers. For liberation theory, therefore, radical change to the structure of society is required in order to end oppression.

Liberation theory is both similar to, and differs from, dependency theory in one significant respect. Unlike dependency theory liberation theory does suggest a mechanism for political change and development and that mechanism is education and in particular political education. However, like dependency theory there is a problem with the ultimate question of the direction of development as, although some form of socialism is often implied, it is not necessarily very clear what the outcome of education for liberation will be nor precisely what the radical restructuring of society will result in.

Perhaps the best known and most influential writer on education for liberation is the Brazilian Paulo Freire (see, for example, Freire, 1972 and 1985). For Freire the essence of education about society is that social reality is made by people and can be changed by people. It is important that learners see that social and political reality is not fixed, immutable and inevitable but that it can be changed and transformed. This is because the social and political reality facing young people in developing countries is most often one of inequality, exploitation and oppression. All too often schools are part of what Freire refers to as a 'culture of silence' where young people are taught to accept what is handed down to them by the ruling elite. Their education aims to socialise them so that they carry out orders from above in an unquestioning and unthinking manner. Their understanding of reality is limited to what they are told to accept and believe – the myths that keep them silent and in ignorance.

Freire argues that instead of this education should be a process of 'conscientisation', of an attempt to raise critical consciousness so that learners both understand their social reality and can act upon it. Education can never be neutral – people are educated either for domestication in an oppressive culture of silence or for liberation through conscientisation. Such an education aims at the development of a frame of mind, a way of thinking, which takes nothing for granted and which emphasises doubt and uncertainty:

> What I learned in exile I would recommend to all readers of this book: each day be open to the world, be ready to think; each day be ready not to accept what is said just because it is said, be predisposed to reread what is read; each day investigate, question and doubt. I think it is most necessary to doubt. I feel it is always necessary not to be sure, that is to be overly sure of certainties. (1985: 181)

Such an education is not compatible with traditional, didactic forms of teaching where the teacher formally transmits factual knowledge from the front and where the learners passively receive it, memorise it and repeat it in examinations. This is sometimes referred to by Freire as 'banking education', whereby knowledge (as defined by the teacher) is 'deposited' in the student and on which he or she is later expected to 'capitalise'. It implies a view of knowledge as static, as made and finished and of learners as empty and lacking consciousness. Freire cites ten ways in which this sort student–teacher relationship manifests itself:

1   The teacher teachers and the students are taught.
2   The teacher knows everything and the students know nothing.
3   The teacher thinks and the students are thought about.
4   The teacher talks and the students listen – meekly.
5   The teacher disciplines and the students are disciplined.
6   The teacher chooses and enforces his or her choice and the students comply.
7   The teacher acts and the students have the illusion of acting through the action of the teacher.
8   The teacher chooses the programme content and the students comply.

9   The teacher confuses the authority of knowledge with professional
    authority which he or she sets in opposition to the freedom of the
    students.
10 The teacher is the subject of the learning process while the pupils
    are mere objects. (Freire, 1972: 46–7)

Critical education, on the other hand, means involving students in
their own learning and interpretation of the world through dialogue,
questioning, participation and discussion.

However, a major problem with Freire is that while the teaching
and learning methods he supports are compatible with education for
democracy there is a problem with outcomes. It often appears from his
writing that there are clear-cut, 'correct' answers to the question of
whether or not there are oppressors, who the oppressors are and what
the way forward should be. Moreover, once these answers have been
established the masses must be 'educated' to see them. The answers to
these questions may be more straightforward in a colonial situation but
in a context where formal political independence has been won they are
a question of value rather that fact. Unfortunately, Freire often appears
to favour the indoctrination of a new orthodoxy as favoured by the
revolutionary party that has liberated the country from colonialism.
Indeed, he has been accused of siding too closely with Amilcar Cabral
and the PAIGC in the West African state of Guinea-Bissau when he
worked there in the 1970s to the point that when the Portuguese
colonialists left and the PAIGC became the sole party of government,
he was prepared to accept Cabral's dictum that the people must
find their political existence and expression through the party and
develop under its tutelage 'because of the economic and cultural
limitation of the masses'. As the writer who makes this point states:

> The contradictions in Freire's theoretical enterprise, within the context
> of subordination of all basic functions to the processes of a single
> organisation, the party, produce the negation of some of his most
> basic ideals . . . Conscientisation as cultural action for liberation is
> ultimately impossible unless the implicitly authoritarian model of
> political leadership is jettisoned . . . (Walker, 1980: 146)

Democratisation Theory and Re-schooling

Such contradictions in Freire's thought pose problems for those who
support a genuine education for democracy. While much, if not all,
of what Freire has to say about educational method is consistent with
education for democracy, the problem arises in relation to the goal of

such an education. If there is a predetermined 'answer' to education for critical consciousness, the correctness of the post-colonial party and its version of socialism, then much of what Freire has to say about doubt, uncertainty, investigation, questioning and dialogue is rendered meaningless. What is required in the light of the 'return to democracy' and the renewed interest in political culture described above is thinking that retains Freire's valuable insights into the political nature of education and the need for critical educational method but which resolves this contradiction in terms of the purpose of such an education. A number of political scientists are now working on the wider theories and issues surrounding the democratising of political institutions and processes in developing countries (see, for example, Diamond, 1993) but it is up to educationalists to contribute to the debate at the level of partial or sub-theory by adding education as an important piece of the jigsaw of overall democratisation. If this sub-theory requires a label then an adaptation of Ivan Illich's (1971) phrase 'de-schooling' to 're-schooling' would seem appropriate.

This book examines both the present role of schooling in hindering the process of democratisation in Africa and its future potential for assisting it. A consistent theme throughout it is that education for democracy is as much about the way in which people think and behave, how they hold their political opinions, than what they actually think. Education for democracy, therefore, does not therefore assume a predetermined outcome. The aim of political education for democracy is not, for example, to create conservatives or socialists but rather that people should decide their political opinions for themselves on the basis of informed judgement. This would mean that political learning in schools would move from the common situation now where pupils learn preferences and predispositions towards certain political values and attitudes rather than others, even though often in a context where other viewpoints may be available, to a genuine political education where there is an attempt to create critical awareness of political phenomena by open, balanced discussion and analysis of a range of evidence and opinions.

The political opinions that resulted from such a political education are unpredictable and should be held in a manner which is not dogmatic but which is open-minded and subject to a degree of uncertainty, for as Thomas Robert Dewar the American writer put it 'Minds are like parachutes: they only function when they are open'. To which can be added the psychologist Carl Rogers' observation that 'People who can't think are ripe for dictatorships' (both quoted in Meighan, 1994). The chapters that follow will argue that education for democracy based on these ideas is a radical departure from the authoritarian nature of most current practice, and will explore its practical implications for both curriculum and school organisation and management in Africa.

Conclusion

This chapter has discussed the contribution of theory to issues of education and political development. In particular it has focused on the question of destination – education for what sort of political system and for what sort of citizens? The attempt to be 'neutral' in defining development in terms of rates of participation led political modernisation theorists to devalue democracy as a political goal and instead to emphasise stability and order. This led to education being perceived as an instrument of modernisation in the sense of bureaucratic socialisation. More recently there has been a return to a concern for democracy as the goal of political development and a renewed interest in the nature of the political culture supportive of democracy. This has changed the focus of the debate from simply participation to the ways in which citizens participate in a democracy and the type of education necessary for such citizenship. Liberation theory has been particularly helpful in this regard and it is now important to think about how formal education can be re-schooled to educate for democracy.

4

Authoritarian Schooling in Africa

Schools in most parts of the world (Harber, 1991, 1995) are presently essentially authoritarian institutions. Power over curriculum and management is hierarchically organised with the Ministry at the top, the headteacher next and the teachers third in terms of control. Pupils play little part in school processes other than as receivers of rules and information. Ball's case studies of British schools, for example, found that the political model is authoritarian with the headteacher at the top of a hierarchical chain of command. The role of the teachers in this model is that, while they are 'consulted' about policy, this is not regarded as binding by headteachers and teachers have no real access to decision making. Rather these 'rights of participation' are a political ritual which lends support to what is in reality a system of autocracy (Ball, 1987: 125–6).

Charles Handy, a writer on business organisations, has gone further and compared secondary schools to prisons in their organisational style in that the inmates' work routine is disrupted every forty minutes, they change their place of work and supervisors constantly, they have no place to call their own and they are often forbidden to communicate and co-operate with each other. In another way schools are like factories and the pupils are like products which are inspected at the end of the production line, sometimes rejected as sub-standard and then stamped 'history', 'maths', 'science' and so on. Handy's survey of schools also asked the teachers in the schools, 'How many people are there in this organisation? They answered ten or seventy or whatever – they nearly always left out the pupils (Handy, 1984).

This authoritarian nature of schooling in Africa is clearly observable at the level of the classroom. Datta (1984: 40) describes the situation thus:

> In most African countries the classroom is highly structured in terms of the formal distribution of space. The teacher in the classroom exercises unquestioned authority in such matters as seating arrangement and movement. He not only initiates the activities to be pursued by pupils,

but also controls communication channels within the group. We do not know the extent to which this kind of classroom environment determines the political orientation of pupils but forced conformity to an authoritarian system throughout childhood and early adolescence, if supplemented by other factors, is likely to encourage passive acceptance of authority in later years.

This general statement is supported by evidence from individual African countries. In Nigeria DuBey et al. (1979: 37) describe headteachers as authoritarian if not altogether autocratic; and Harber (1989: ch. 5) argues that the evidence is that schools socialise towards authoritarianism with the result that pupils possess political values in keeping with what Almond and Verba (1963) term a 'subject political culture' where citizens play little part in government, are subject only to the administrative, output side of the political system and where there is a top-down flow of information and an emphasis on obedience and compliance. In Malawi, according to Fuller (1991: 45), teachers hold as sacred certain pedagogical practices and forms of knowledge such as lecturing to pupils and exercising hierarchical authority. He uses the example of a teacher in a school in Malawi going through the script laid out in the national textbook. The curriculum writers had included 'questions to encourage discussion' so this teacher simply had the pupils shout out the questions in unison – the teacher did not realise that these were queries to be debated rather than additional material simply to be recited (1991: 45, 63).

Even in Tanzania, despite the philosophy of education for self-reliance, classrooms still tend to be authoritarian and this is characterised by the 'copy-copy' teaching method where the teacher copies sections from a textbook or notebook onto the blackboard and pupils copy these notes into their own notebooks. Mbilinyi (1979: 1–7) notes that these methods are typical of Freire's 'banking' approach to teaching, 'where the teacher controls the content of the lesson and perceives his work to be filling up the heads of his students with his own knowledge, disregarding whatever knowledge they may have and also disregarding their ability to investigate knowledge on their own'.

The remainder of this chapter explores the question of why schools in Africa are authoritarian in terms of school organisation, the interpretation of knowledge and the role of culture.

School Organisation

When mass schooling was introduced in Europe towards the end of the nineteenth century it was based on the then predominant model of commercial and industrial organisation – bureaucracy. This is characterised by hierarchy, order, rule imposition, appointment rather than election and secrecy. Max Weber, historically the most influential writer on bureaucracy, was clear that it is a form of domination (Ball, 1987: 101–3).

Schools were organised bureaucratically to teach the impersonal, contractual values and relationships that typify the transition from agricultural to industrial society. Thus the values that were reinforced in the school are those which are needed for the functioning of bureaucratic organisation and the maintenance of social order – obedience, abiding by the rules, loyalty, respect for authority, punctuality, regular attendance, quietness, orderly work in large groups, response to orders, bells and timetables, tolerance of monotony, the ability to change from one situation to the next and the ignoring of personal needs when these are irrelevant to the task in hand (Shipman, 1971: ch. 2).

The rigid and bureaucratic nature of such schooling is nicely captured in a poem by a seventeen-year-old pupil from Ghana entitled 'The Supreme Bell':

> The week begins with a bell.
> Morning assembly begins with a bell.
> Lessons begin with a bell.
> Prep-time, where the seniors bully us, begins with the bell.
>
> Annoying role-call starts with the bell.
> Games start with the bell.
> For three academic years
> I shall be a slave to the bell.
> Happy will I be when I say goodbye
> to the Supreme Bell.
>
> (BBC *Focus on Africa*, Oct.–Dec. 1994)

When schools were established in in the colonial territories this authoritarian-bureaucatic organisational model was transported from Europe in order to inculcate the skills and values necessary to provide the subordinate African personnel required for the effective functioning of the colonial administration. In the post-colonial period the existence in Africa of what Fuller, writing on Malawi, terms 'fragile states' which lack deeply-rooted legitimacy, especially in rural areas where the majority of the population lives, means that governments must attempt to enhance their shallow authority by appearing 'modern'. One important way of doing this is persistently to signal to the population the existence and constant extension of meritocracy and mass opportunity. Schools as government institutions signal and symbolise modernity and must therefore be organised in a 'modern', bureaucratic way:

> The younger, more fragile state, common across the Third World, plays a much stronger role in importing and legitimating the bureaucratic structure and moral order of the Western school. Bureaucratic administration signals 'modern practice', particularly in societies where rationalised organisations or firms are still a novel form. Here the visible contours and symbols of 'modern organisation' take on enormous power. The Third World school may fail to hold deep effects on children's acquired literacy or secular values. But the fact that the school is tightly administered – with tidy accounts, a sharp schedule of classes and attractive gardens – signals the attributes of modern organisation. The institution is recognised by local parents as a concrete instrument of modernity, even if the school's technical objective of raising literacy is rarely accomplished. (Fuller, 1991: 43–4)

Moreover, the ministerial bureaucracies of states in Africa, learning from their colonial administrators, often attempt to manage schooling through strict, centralised regimes. This promotes educational forms and processes that are inherently undemocratic and bureaucratic because, as Carnoy and Samoff (1990: 93) argue, 'it is precisely such forms that strengthen the control of a centralised bureaucracy over teachers and students'. The result is a definition of knowledge and curriculum which is top-down and highly centralised.

Not surprisingly therefore, that:

> Throughout Africa . . . lessons involve frequent oral recitation of vocabulary or arithmetic exercises, delivered in unison by all pupils. This mechanical process, set by the curricula or teacher guide, helps control and engage the fifty to ninety restless pupils that commonly sit before the teacher. Thus curricular content helps signal and legitimate certain forms of authority and human interaction which come to be seen as normal in a modern (hierarchical) organisation. (Fuller, 1991: 68)

With the introduction of school authoritarianism came a further instrument of its imposition and maintenance – the cane. Unfortunately, this is still widely used in African schools. In her study of teachers in Zimbabwe, for example, Davies (1993: 167) quotes a headline from the *Financial Gazette* (23 March 1990) 'Son canned at St. John's College'. The letter went on to say 'My son was canned after four days at St. John's College for failing a French test . . . five weeks later the bruises were still visible . . . the headmaster admitted the canning was a mistake'. The ensuing correspondence about the case was interesting in its greater concern about the spelling than about the corporal punishment itself: the latter was less unusual. A further letter from a pupil complaining that he was caned every morning for being late because of transport problems (in spite of getting up at 5 a.m.)

resulted in the newspaper evoking a reply from the transport company rather than any discussion of the appropriateness of the punishment. As the Tanzanian writer Mbilinyi (1979) argues, the use of the cane is more symbolic of the relationship between oppressor and oppressed than the relationship based on respect between co-operating equals desired in a democracy. This is why Namibia has recently banned the use of the cane in all of its schools.

In chapter 7, on schools as democratic organisations, it will be argued that a more democratically organised school is a more effective school than an authoritarian bureaucracy. Here it is important to note the words of Handy and Aitken in their book *Understanding Schools as Organisations*:

> Interestingly, however, modern businesses are moving away from hierarchies towards networks in response to the need for more flexibility and in order to give more room to the individual. It may be that in aping the bureaucracy of large businesses the secondary school has been adopting a theory of management that is already out of date. (1986: 95)

School Knowledge

Schooling in Africa tends to be based on an epistemology or view of knowledge as certain, factual and objective rather than contentious and subject to change and interpretation. Kelly (1986) describes how this view of knowledge stems from European culture at the end of the eighteenth century, the period of the 'Enlightenment'. The aim at the time was to formulate general laws based on observation and experiment. Kelly quotes the philosopher Isiah Berlin on this period: 'To every genuine question there were many false answers and only one true one; once discovered it was final – it remained forever true; all that was needed was a reliable method of discovery.' This applied not only to the material world of the natural sciences but also to the social and political world of human beings where it was therefore possible to treat people as though they were objects and therefore to find 'factual' solutions to social problems and indeed to create the perfect, utopian society.

Kelly has argued that this 'rationalist' view of knowledge with its stress on certainty and the 'right' answer necessarily leads to authoritarianism in many spheres of life – the moral, the political and the educational. This is because if knowledge is absolute and unchanging then there cannot be legitimate alternatives to it. There is little point in discussion and dialogue as the role of the teacher is to impart a factual body of knowledge to a body of immature recipients. This means a stress on knowledge/subject matter rather than on the learner, and also leads to a hierarchy of those that 'know' (the teachers) and those that don't (the pupils). It was this view of knowledge and learning that was exported to Africa by missionaries in the nineteenth and twentieth centuries.

Serpell (1993), writing on Zambia, describes the formal education which resulted as a 'condescending process' in which the teacher has an obligation to control and direct the student along a pre-determined path. There is an asymmetry in the flow of information between teacher and pupil and classroom activities are strictly controlled by the teacher so that any deviation by a pupil from prescribed forms of behaviour is subject to authoritarian correction. This condescending style of teaching, compounded at the time by an ethnocentric assumption of cultural superiority, has remained a salient feature of schooling even in those schools run by local teachers employed by the government so that it has become almost a local or regional educational tradition. Serpell notes that the resulting

> style of classroom management favoured in most African schools still resembles the 'chalk and talk' model of early twentieth century Western schools. Largely content-free drills are used pervasively to impart much of the curriculum, with an apparent rationale of memorisation. Progress is assessed by the criterion of accurate recitation of the alphabet, the times-table and 'factual' lesson-notes copied from the blackboard into exercise books. Moreover, most teachers administer their classes in a highly directive ('didactic') manner, demanding deferential silence from their students except when called upon to answer specific questions, and enforcing the adherence to rigid procedural routines with authoritarian discipline. (1993: 93–4)

He comments that no one asked, when exporting European education to Africa, how African societies conceptualise children and their educational needs. Instead, a set of interdependent equations deeply ingrained in the practices of Western education were exported to Africa. These were:

civilisation = urban life-style
education = schooling
intelligence = aptitude for school subjects

While these were exported under the label of opportunities for enlightenment, liberation and enrichment, in practice they often served the opposite purposes of mystification, oppression and impoverishment (1993: 106).

The opposite of this traditional, rationalist view of knowledge is what Kelly (1986) describes as 'empiricist'. In this epistemology knowledge comes only into the human mind through contact between the human senses and the material and social world. Because knowledge cannot be independent of the knower, it cannot be certain and thus knowledge is tentative and hypothetical. Knowledge is made by individuals and is socially constructed by human beings. The tentative, uncertain and problematic nature of knowledge meant that education had to be viewed as learner-centred rather than subject or knowledge-centred. Kelly notes that education therefore had to 'see the development of the individual as the central concern of education and the selection of knowledge content as subsidiary and subordinate to that' (1986: 7).

While the rationalist view of knowledge with its authoritarian educational implications has been the predominant model both in colonial and post-colonial Africa, there have been exceptions. The earliest was that of 'education for self-reliance' launched by the then president of Tanzania, Julius Nyerere, in 1967. This was a conscious and deliberate rejection of colonial forms of schooling and an attempt to challenge the three equations listed above by a closer integration of schooling and African life and culture. It was empirical in that Nyerere wanted education grounded in practice and experience, and in particular the practice and experience of the predominant form of employment in the country – agriculture. Not only would pupils get first-hand experience of working in the 'shamba' or agricultural plot attached to the school but also academic lessons would be integrated with agricultural or other productive experience. In other words learning would become active, participant, problem-solving and practical whatever the curriculum subject. This is more fully discussed in relation to the implications for democratic school structures in Tanzania in chapter 7. More recently a philosophy of learner-centred education has been adopted by the government of Namibia and this is fully discussed in chapter 8.

Culture

A third factor contributing to the prevalence of authoritarian schools in many parts of Africa has been traditional political cultures and patterns of child-rearing. While such cultures can be termed 'traditional' in that they have existed for a long period of time, they are of considerable importance in understanding the contemporary nature of modern African states. This section examines examples of case studies of two such cultures in terms of their implications for education and democracy – the Hausa/Fulani culture of northern Nigeria and the Tswana culture of Botswana.

Diamond (1988b), in discussing the progress of democracy in Nigeria since independence in 1960, notes both the dominance of the northern Hausa/Fulani in both civilian and military periods of politics, and the general ethnic and political intolerance and repression that has marked political life. The nature of traditional Hausa political culture is therefore an important factor in the future of democracy in Nigeria as a whole, yet key aspects of Hausa culture do not seem to sit comfortably with the values supportive of a democracy. This was and is a steeply hierarchical system in which the role of the citizen is seen in terms of loyalty, obedience and dependence on those in authority. It is a system that favours qualities of servility, respect for authority and allegiance to the powerful, and rejects qualities of independent achievement, self-reliant action and initiative (Le Vine 1966; Paden 1973).

Eleazu (1977: 65–6) argued that family-rearing patterns in northern Nigeria, which is predominantly Islamic, reflect the Islamic idea that people are in need of a hierarchical ordering of roles and he states that 'from early childhood it is drummed into the child that obedience to the powers-that-be is the first duty of a person'. In a study of child-rearing practices in northern Nigeria, Hake found that fear was the dominant means that adults used to control youngsters, relying heavily on corporal punishment to induce respect, humility, obedience and submission. He notes that, in general, fear of punishment rather than positive reinforcement of good behaviour, appears to be the dominant method of helping children learn proper behavioural controls. These fears eventually establish life patterns of servile submission to authority which extend into adulthood (1972: 41–2).

The Hausa child's experience of authority in the family is similar to that experienced in the Koranic school. It is usual for Hausa children to experience some Koranic education before attendance at primary school and many will continue with it at primary school by going to Koranic schools in the late afternoon and evening. As in the family, there is an emphasis on physical punishment, obedience and deference (Skinner, 1977; Sanneh, 1975). Hiskett (1975) characterises as authoritarian the pedagogical style common to both Koranic schools for the young and the schools for higher Islamic learning for those who have achieved a certain proficiency in memorising the Koran. Teaching is based on rote learning and the uncritical acceptance of a transmitted body of knowledge without argument or disagreement.

The political values of the Hausa family and the Koranic school, while they may not be 'modern' in a bureaucratic sense, are nevertheless congruent with the hierarchical authoritarianism of the imported western model of education. In this sense traditional Hausa culture and western schooling have posed no real threat to each other and in terms of authority patterns have been mutually supportive.

In Botswana, on the other hand, the emphases in traditional Tswana culture on moderation, non-violence and obedience to the law as well as public discussion and community consensus, have facilitated and helped to sustain democratic government. However, while these values have been helpful in supporting democratic government:

> In some respects they compensate for the lack of rigorous support for the legal rights of speech and press already mentioned . . . there is little in the traditional culture that supports the idea of the popular election of leaders. There is a presumption, particularly in the rural areas, that males from the royal family ought to rule. As a consequence, outside the cities, the public shows little concern about the central government's appointments to local councils. It is presumed that the central government has the real power, that it is the new chief. It is hard to say yet that this system of leadership is 'deeply institutionalised', given the fact that several centuries of autocratic political practice predated the present regime. (Holm, 1988: 198, 202)

Furthermore, traditional child-rearing practices have not necessarily been helpful in the further development of a political culture that fosters democratic citizenship, being characterised by domination and subordination of the child and the development of a dependent mode of thinking (Tabulawa, 1995). This pattern of domination and subordination comes directly from the social importance accorded to age in Tswana culture for 'any senior of the same sex is one's superior and junior of the same sex one's subordinate' (Alverson, 1978: 13). Traditionally, Tswana society was ranked by age sets or age regiments in which one remained throughout one's life. These were deferential to age sets of their seniors and expected the same from junior age sets.

The importance of age is explained by Alverson (1978) in terms of the concepts of time and ageing in Tswana cosmology. Age has its basis in a set of ancestral relationships. Ageing, seen as a movement towards death, is simultaneously a movement towards the ancestors and therefore the origins of the society. Age is defined in terms of nearness to the ancestors and the accumulation of experience. Although children and adults share a closeness to the final order of the ancestors, one having recently come from there and one on its way there, wisdom is the prerequisite of the adults because of accumulated knowledge and experience. This puts the child in an inherently subordinate position as the child must always learn from the elders. This is so because for the Tswana knowledge is 'remembering things past' (Alverson, 1978: 171) and compared to adults children have little to remember. As a result the Tswana feel that there is very little of value that an elder can learn from his or her junior. Therefore:

> Much of the child training consists in imparting the etiquette that an older individual (doing the instructing) feels should govern how a junior person acts towards a senior person. Basically this is training in deference . . . The Tswana are rigid and authoritarian disciplinarians who enjoy teaching legalistic do's and dont's in manners of public decorum, etiquette and role obligations . . . Child training is directed towards producing a mannerly, conforming and industrious person. (Alverson, 1978: 68)

As in Nigeria, schools in Botswana reinforce these patterns of child-rearing. Alverson (1978) sees formal education as a perfect reflection of Tswana patterns of child-rearing involving rote learning, punishment for mistakes and errors. Creativity, self-reliance and autonomy are discouraged as students must display docility, obedience and submissiveness. Rowell and Prophet, for example, studied science classrooms in Botswana and concluded that:

> Students are perceived as passive recipients of vast amounts of information to be memorised and as apprentices in the acquisition of elementary skills required for the production of specific products. Learning is perceived to occur through repetition and drill, the effectiveness of which is assessed through the use of test questions requiring little more than simple recall. (1990: 24)

However, it is important not to be too deterministic about the nature of political culture and its patterns of child-rearing. Rather a more malleable, 'plastic' or changeable view of political culture both shaping and being shaped by state and society is required. One main reason for this is what Diamond (1993: 9–10) terms a 'bias towards hope', i.e. that to see political cultures as fixed and unchanging would be to condemn many countries in the developing world and the ex-communist bloc to perpetual authoritarianism and praetorianism. This would not only be deeply pessimistic but is contradicted by the real and enduring change in countries such as Germany, Japan, Spain, Italy and Portugal which were once written off as infertile ground for democracy. Buddy Wentworth, the Deputy Minister of Education in Namibia, has stressed the need to create a 'culture of human rights and democracy' in Namibia:

> We no longer have the luxury of providing our children and their families with knowledge about and motivations toward peace, human rights and democracy. We face now the necessary present challenge of finding ways directly to change destructive values and images of

our fellow humans. We must find ways to create measurable change in the behaviour of learners, not just an increase of knowledge. Our emphasis is no longer on cognitive learning alone, but on affective and behavioural learning as well. (Undated: 4)

Conclusion

Two broad factors have helped to establish the authoritarian nature of schooling in much of Africa today – the model of schooling and knowledge imported with colonialism and its interaction with existing cultures. Moreover, this model has become established in the minds of many participants – parents, teachers, pupils, policy makers, employers – as 'the' model of school to which no alternative exists. It is too often perceived in its present shape as natural, given and unalterable rather than as a social construction largely stemming from a particular period. Something that is socially constructed, however, can be reconstructed, though the process will inevitably be difficult.

The present educational structures have within them many features which tend to reproduce the unvirtuous authoritarian cycle. Tradition, for example, is a powerful force so that teachers teach as they were taught and teacher trainers train according to the traditional model. Schools have always been primarily about 'facts' so examinations test memorisation of knowledge and this in turn has a backwash effect on teaching and learning methods which remain didactically insistent on transmitting the facts rather than developing skills or exploring values. Perhaps most of all the political willpower has been absent – African governments in the recent past have not necessarily wanted independent, critical and confident citizens, though this situation is now changing in certain parts of the continent. The next chapter examines some of these obstacles to democratic education in more detail in relation to one key curriculum area – social studies.

5

Education for Democracy? Curriculum and Reality in African Social Studies Education

> Do we teach our youth to question or conform? It was over a question of curriculum that Socrates drank hemlock. (Hawes, 1979: 1)

Of all the subjects most commonly found in the curriculum of formal schooling, social studies is the one that most directly and explicitly has as its aim the study of society. This endows social studies with considerable potential for the critical examination of a whole range of social and political structures, processes, organisations and beliefs. One Nigerian writer, for example, states that:

> Thus as Paulo Freire says, Social Studies offers the individual 'critical consciousness', the highest level of conscientization process. The term conscientization refers to learning to perceive social, political and economic contradictions and to take action against the oppressive elements of reality. (Akintola, 1980: 8)

This chapter explores the role of social studies in African schools in creating citizens who are critically aware of the social realities surrounding them and who possess the skills and proclivities necessary for social and political action. As the title suggests, a major theme is one that is examined by Hawes (1979) in relation to the whole curriculum – the gap between the social studies curriculum and the reality of schooling. This chapter therefore also identifies some of the major curricular obstacles to education for democracy in Africa through the case study of social studies.

African Social Studies Programmes

The organisation that has most influenced the development of social studies in Africa (especially Anglophone Africa) is the ASSP. This co-ordinating body for social studies education was set up in 1969 and has representatives from seventeen different African countries – Botswana, Ethiopia, Gambia, Ghana, Kenya, Lesotho, Liberia, Malawi, Nigeria, Sierra Leone, Somalia, Sudan, Swaziland, Tanzania, Uganda, Zambia and Zimbabwe. It encourages member countries to initiate social studies programmes in their respective countries by organising seminars, conferences and workshops on new trends in the subject; by organising workshops for the development of social studies curricula, textbooks and materials; by providing liaison services for the exchange of curriculum materials developed by member countries; by soliciting research on social studies education; and by disseminating information through its journal, the African Social Studies Forum. The ASSP is based in Nairobi, where it has a resource centre containing documentation on social studies education in the member countries. This documentation (syllabuses, ASSP publications, school textbooks, conference reports, etc.) served as a major source of information for this chapter. The aims and objectives of the ASSP have been summarised as follows:

> That every school-going child in Africa shall be given the opportunity, through social studies education, to acquire the knowledge and to develop the skills, attitudes and values that will enable him:
>
> (a) to identify his personality as an African with a heritage worthy of pride, preservation and improvement;
> (b) to grow up conscious of his capabilities and eager to contribute to the survival of himself and his society;
> (c) to relate effectively with others in his community and his country, and with others in Africa and the rest of the world.
>
> That every school-going child in Africa shall be given the opportunity to learn about the social and physical environment without inhibition of subject area restrictions.
> That every school-going child in Africa shall discover knowledge through enquiry, self-involvement and practical activity. In particular the African school child shall be given the opportunity through social studies education to:
>
> (a) discover knowledge with the guidance of the teacher;
> (b) apply problem-solving techniques to new learning situations;
> (c) train his mind in building valuable concepts and generalisations for the purpose of understanding the world around him;
> (d) develop skills that will enable him to solve environmental problems and control and improve his environment effectively;
> (e) become development conscious.
>
> (ASSP 1985)

A close observer of the work of the ASSP summarises it as being in favour not only of integration, enquiry method, putting the local before the national and international, national building and the contribution of teachers and students to local curriculum development, but also (and despite the gender bias in the language of its aims and objectives) the 'skills and attitudes of citizens in a free and democratic society' (i.e. discovery, critical thinking, problem-solving). However, the same observer also notes that in practice problems of isolation and ignorance often mean that most people in the new states accept the status quo and remain unaware of the possibilities which could improve their lives (Merryfield, 1986: 5, 78–9).

Indeed the publications of the ASSP show considerable sympathy with a Freirean analysis of the status quo that constitutes social reality. At an ASSP seminary on Peace Education, International Understanding and Human Rights, for example, a proposed syllabus for the upper primary school had as one of its aims the elimination of 'human exploitation in all its forms' and the prevention of 'gross disparities in individual work, income and the growth of social classes', while at the same seminar the then executive secretary of the ASSP stated that:

> There is discrimination between urban and rural populations, between the sexes, between the rich and the poor, between the children from illiterate homes, between the physically fit and the disabled children, between the closely related children and the children of others. The challenge to education is really great – human problems/weakness can frustrate the best plans for education. If we desire peace,inequality must be solved as an important problem. Discrimination in education in Africa is a basic factor which encourages inequality and therefore unhappiness,violence, conflict and war. (ASSP, 1979: 22, 35)

But the ASSP is optimistic, in that its creation and its journal 'evolved directly from the notion that social studies curriculum has the power to change nations' (Barth, 1986: vii).

However, while the ASSP itself is committed to social studies as critical reflection on social reality and the development of skills of social action, to what extent is this potential actually being achieved in the member states? The first edition of *Forum* sounds the cautionary note that social studies education can in reality either function as an instrument of oppression or liberation. What are the constraints and problems facing a critical social studies education in African schools? What factors inhibit the development of critical social studies?

The Political Environment

The free exploration and investigation of social reality which might result in criticism and dissent is a sensitive matter in any society.

In Africa, it is particularly difficult because the surrounding political systems have rarely been geared to democratic political values. Thus, two of the five main objectives for education in Nigeria (the country in Africa where social studies is perhaps most developed) are 'a free and democratic society' and 'a just and egalitarian society'; but these do not sit easily with the existing conditions of military government, the absence of elections and some official violence against citizens. Indeed, of the seventeen countries that were members of the ASSP in 1987, only two, Botswana and The Gambia, had no limitations on the right to vote and no record of official violence against citizens (Sivard, 1987: 27).

Even where African social studies syllabuses include reference to such procedural values as honesty, tolerance, open-mindedness, social awareness, critical judgement, fairness or justice (e.g. in this case, Nigeria), they must be treated with a certain amount of caution because they will have to be interpreted and mediated by teachers. In a predominantly authoritarian political framework, teachers of social studies are at the least going to feel concerned about handling controversial issues and are unlikely to be predisposed to permit unfettered and free discussion of the party, president, key policies and established, widespread social customs. Indeed, even where the political environment has seemed temporarily favourable, there is still political instability and unpredictability for the teacher to contend with.

Moreover, curricular aims sometimes contain tensions and contradictions, as Hawes notes in relation to Malawi under President Banda:

> The 'four cornerstones' of the Malawi Congress Party: unity, loyalty, obedience and discipline, match ill with the 'scientific spirit of enquiry' which the country's 1966 syllabus announces as the guiding principle for primary education syllabus change. (1979: 35)

Even in those sets of aims for social studies that do espouse democratic values there are often values stressed which sit uneasily next to them (e.g. obedience/obedience to authority, social harmony, the need to adjust to society and patriotism). It would take courageous teachers, therefore (as well as well-trained ones), to implement the values of the ASSP too literally.

There is less ambiguity in some countries of the ASSP as little reference is made to open, critical values in social studies. In Ethiopia under the Mengistu regime, for example, the concern was with 'moulding a new man' according to a particular socialist model:

> Socialist society demands the development of a particular personality, which fits only the socialist system . . . In social studies education high priority has been given to ideological education. This education is directed towards developing elements of socialist consciousness and motivating corresponding modes of behaviour. (Alaro, 1985: 32–3)

This reinforces the point that the practical question of teaching method should not be confused with the underlying aims and purposes of the classroom. Ethiopia was keen to promote more participant classroom methods, but this was in order to achieve a better understanding of the official ideology rather than to critically examine it, its achievements and shortcomings, and Ethiopian society in general. The tension between open discussion and a socialist perspective has also existed in Tanzania and leads to teachers being reluctant to handle controversial issues in the classroom for fear of trouble with the authorities (Mgulambwa et al., 1985).

In other countries, too, while reference may be made to desirable aims in regard to social studies, there is little emphasis on education for critical consciousness. To take an example of a more conservative country, Malawi, the aims of history, geography and civics (social studies is not taught as an integrated subject) have been very much about the provision of information rather than critical thought and participation (e.g. 'understanding the way we depend on one another by showing how life in the local district is influenced by co-operation among the people in it', 'know how countryside and town are interdependent', 'study information accurately', 'make accurate reconstruction of the past', 'inculcate in the pupil civic responsibilities', etc.). Moreover, this factual/neutral approach (which is basically conservative because it simply reproduces the status quo) is reflected in the opinions of teachers and district education personnel in Malawi about why these subjects are included in the primary school curriculum (Merryfield, 1986: 535).

In The Gambia, where a more democratic political environment existed for some time, the primary social studies course does recognise that social studies involves the formation of a range of opinions and values, but also tends to retreat quickly into stressing the 'factual' as much as possible rather than suggesting ways of handling controversial issues in the classroom: 'Even more delicate is the way you (the teachers) treat the facts you have collected. Your presentation now could have unforeseen repercussions twenty years hence. Your aim should be to present the facts and avoid giving opinions as much as you can' (The Gambia Primary Course, 1984: 2).

The syllabus maintains a democratic stance in its opposition to military coups but tends to lump all forms of protest together in a way that both tends to foreclose debate and give the impression (perhaps understandably given the wider political context of West Africa) that stability rather than democracy is the aim.

During the last four or five years the political environment in Africa has improved dramatically with most states experiencing free elections. However, Africa is still in a very early stage of democratic transition and, as we saw in chapter 2, there are already signs in countries like Nigeria and Kenya of a return to authoritarianism. Moreover, in 1994 Gambia itself experienced a military coup. Social and political education is in the paradoxical position that it requires a reasonably democratic environment in which to exist but can only slowly contribute to the development of a political culture that will support and sustain democracy in the longer term.

Teaching Materials

Teaching materials, and in particular textbooks, are very influential in defining the view of the world portrayed in the social studies classroom. Teachers in Africa, as elsewhere, regard them as the starting point for classroom method and, as will be discussed below, the shortage of such books is a major complaint of teachers in many African countries. The present concern, however, is with the content of teaching materials.

If pupils are going to engage in critical discussion it is important that, at the very least, social studies textbooks reflect the social reality of the surrounding society. This is not always the case. The Nigerian Secondary Schools Social Studies Project replaced the ubiquitous Aiyetoro High School textbook in 1979 and has been reprinted three times, in 1981, 1983 and 1984. It is marked by the sin of omission. Page 1 of Book 1 begins by saying that, 'It would not be very useful to study social studies if it did not help to solve some of the problems of society'. However, these problems are rarely identified in the text, let alone tackled. On page 5, for example, there is a picture of a bulldozer clearing an area of slums, but there is no discussion of who lives in slums, why and what might be done about it. On page 8 there are pictures of an oil refinery and a dam, but nowhere is there any discussion of why their products are often in short supply to consumers. Traditional male/female roles are described, on pages 22 and 28, but the issue of gender inequality is not considered. The whole of chapter 5 is about the need of tolerance and unity, but inter-ethnic mistrust and hostility, including the civil war, is not mentioned even to condemn it. Page 55 makes the point that theft is wrong, but there is no discussion of why it occurs, who commits what type of crime and what might be done about it. Generally the book presents a bland and rosy picture and fails to deal with the realities of Nigerian life.

The above can be contrasted with the Sierra Leone National Programme in Social Studies with Population Education (1984). The tone of the three books that constitute the project is more realistic. The following examples concerning education and youth are from Book 3:

> You know how difficult it is to get accommodation in school for young children, especially in the urban areas of Sierra Leone. (p. 85)

> Give some instances of problems of social adjustment among your schoolmates and state how they may be understood and dealt with. (p. 88)

> Discuss the problems of teenage pregnancy and find out about an organisation which exists in Sierra Leone to help prevent such an occurrence. (p. 89)

An example from Swaziland shows how the external political environment can also influence the content of teaching materials. South Africa and apartheid represented a clear case of oppression and the need for liberation. Yet the geographical (and hence political/economic) position of Swaziland meant that when the topic of South Africa was dealt with in social studies textbooks it is treated with extreme caution, questions of apartheid and political and economic inequality are not discussed. Book 6 of the Swaziland Primary School Social Studies Series has thirteen pages on South Africa, which contain the following statements:

> South Africa is a republic because the head of Government is elected by the people (p. 18).

> At times, as children we do not realise all the help that South Africa offers countries in southern Africa. (p. 27)

> Do you know how the homelands started? These homelands were started so that each African nation could develop its own area in its own way. In the homelands the blacks who have won their own independence, as in Transkei, run their own affairs. (p. 29)

This benevolent view of South Africa is explained by two other statements:

> Our country, Swaziland, and the nearby countries of Lesotho and Botswana buy many of our goods from South Africa. One important reason for this is that these countries are completely surrounded by land and they do not have outlets to the sea. (p. 26)

> Many Swazis work in South Africa . . . (p. 23)

This approach can be contrasted with a social studies handbook for teachers in Zambia:

> The white people can travel everywhere but Africans cannot travel easily. Why is it difficult for Africans to travel freely? (Remind them about apartheid in South Africa, UDI in Rhodesia and Humanism in

Zambia). How are these ideas different from each other? . . . It is a good country for white people to live in, but life is difficult for Africans and other people. (Zambia Ministry of Education, 1977: 46)

Some social studies syllabuses seem to be designed explicitly for social control. One is the Social Education and Ethics course (Kenya Institute of Education, 1987), which has recently become a compulsory subject in all secondary schools in Kenya. It stemmed from the Gachathi Report of 1976 and is designed to combat what Kenyans see as the problems caused by urbanisation, economic change and social dislocation. The course attempts to replace disappearing traditional moral values with an ethical code for modern Kenya. Unfortunately, ethics and morals are often culturally specific and highly subjective. The result is a course which does not aim to explore Kenyan society critically and to promote discussion of social and political issues and structures in an open-minded manner. Rather than supporting such procedural values as respect for evidence and reason, toleration, fairness, etc. it is a prescriptive course which aims to instil notions of what is morally acceptable to the authors. The emphasis is on what the individual needs to be like to be an acceptable member of society. This leads to the course including many subjective social values and viewpoints which are presented as 'correct' rather than as a matter for discussion. The following examples are from the chapter on The Family in the Teachers' Guide to the course:

> Marriage is an institution that belongs to the natural order (p. 18).

> young people as well as adults should be helped to practice the virtue of chastity . . . Outside marriage chastity means total abstention from the use of sex (p. 26).

> the man is the head of the family and as such he has the duty of representing his family on important family matters . . . Most times the women need to dedicate time to running the home and cannot spare much time to an outside job until the children are grown-up without undermining her family's well-being in some way (p. 29).

The course not only creates models of moral behaviour which contain the substantive values of the writers, but which are counsels of perfection and thus seem unattainable and unrealistic (and if achieved would make the individual concerned insufferable). These examples are from the chapter on The School:

> A student, for instance, has a moral obligation to root out behaviour like drug-taking, drinking alcohol and smoking from among his peers. (p. 101)

> The student gradually develops a spirit of sacrifice. He learns to overcome difficulties which come between him and the goal he wants

to attain. He is not only prepared, for instance, to plunge into freezing cold swimming pool water in his preparation for a swimming gala but he actually does so on a regular basis. This student is slowly developing the virtues of fortitude . . . the student will continue to conquer laziness in his study, to control his temper in dealing with others, to persevere at the tasks that are entrusted to him until he finishes them, to say 'no' to another ice cream which would make it one too many, etc. (p. 104)

The course also has a chapter on human rights which includes the rights of physical security and freedom of opinion. Unfortunately, Kenya has in the past been classified as a country where official violence against citizens is frequent (Sivard, 1987: 27) and even at the time of writing in the mid 1990s there are still international concerns about authoritarian tendencies within the regime despite having had multi-party elections.

Therefore, teaching materials can avoid social realities or give a view of social values and behaviour which is out of touch with the realities and problems that students confront in their daily lives. This gap between social studies and the students' own experience has been noted by Nigerian educationalists, who argue that some of the major problem areas of modern Nigeria such as ethnic groupings, statism, corruption, desperate poverty, hunger, indiscipline, unemployment and under-employment, show the need to give realistic education to those who will help to form the society of the future. Yet what many young people actually see and experience in Nigerian society does not reflect the ideals that are indicated in national education statements and social studies courses (Oroge, 1980: 4; Merryfield, 1986: 582).

The Hidden Curriculum of School Organisation

The critical exploration of social reality is facilitated not only by a favourable macro-political environment but also by a favourable micro-political environment (i.e. the authority structure of both the school and the classroom). The latter will be discussed below. Here we are concerned with the whole school.

As was argued in chapter 4, schools in Africa tend to retain the colonial authority structure – they are the hierarchical authoritarian and bureaucratic rather than participant and democratic. The contradiction between existing school structures and what is required for critical education is brought out in analysis of the position in Lesotho in regard to environmental education:

It should be based on certain principles which are totally lacking in today's schools in Lesotho. Such an approach calls for participatory democracy, freedom, a humanistic approach to authority and discipline . . . The major authority for policy should be in the hands of parents, students, and the school in various proportions depending on the age of the students. This kind of a school would call for a different sort of staff from the present one. (Baliloko and Malie, 1979: 4)

Democratic schools that involve pupils in responsibility for school decision making to varying degrees and in varying ways have been introduced and encouraged in some African countries and these will be discussed in other chapters of this book.

The Classroom

Social studies education, as favoured by the ASSP, envisages a move away from traditional authoritarian teaching methods, which 'did not allow much exchange of knowledge among children' (Loum, 1985: 42). Different methods are necessary for the development of a democratic critical consciousness.

Sets of aims for social studies in Africa now usually make reference to active learning methods. Uganda primary social studies, for example, stresses learning by discovery; problem-solving; questioning and thinking skills; the development of initiative, confidence and resourcefulness; the observation, collection and analysis of data, etc. (Kajubi, 1985). However, sets of aims and objectives are not the only factors shaping reality.

Despite occasional lip-service to inquiry methods in Malawi (Simbeye, 1985), it was unlikely that they would be used in the classroom given the President's known hostility. Since the early 1970s, the government of Malawi has taken a firm stand against progressive teaching methods and child-centred enquiry. President Banda said that 'The so-called methods of teaching which allowed pupils to please themselves, to pick up what they liked and leave out what they did not like, have no room in African society because under ordinary village life children are never left to themselves to do as they please' (Merryfield, 1986: 539, 577).

However, even in countries where there is no official opposition to such methods, the evidence suggests that they are not commonly found in schools. One Ugandan writer reports having been to two conferences in 1984 about social studies, at which there were over 200 teachers. There was overwhelming apprehension and vagueness about social studies methodology. The same writer also summarises the findings of twenty-six dissertations at Makere University during the period

1985–7 that investigated social studies in Ugandan primary schools. Where they report on teaching method, as most do, it is uniformly described as traditional and formal (Odada, 1988). Similarly those who have observed social studies teaching in Nigeria have commented on the emphasis on factual knowledge and formal teaching methods (Obebe, 1980: 26; Oguntosin, 1985: 87). In Lesotho, one observer commented that 'It is obvious that teachers still stand in front of children and tell them everything. This is an approach contrary to the demands of the new syllabus' (Maleri, 1983: 35). Even in Tanzania, where the context of education in general was supposed to have been changed in a favourable direction, the teaching of political education courses is dominated by such teacher-centred methods as lecturing and questioning (Elietinize, 1981: 117). Studies of the teaching of primary social studies throughout Kenya have found a heavy reliance on traditional or 'banking' methods (e.g. Ochieng-Moya, 1985: 68; Kabau, 1983: 156; Wasanga, 1987: 65; Merryfield, 1986: 89). Why do these traditional methods persist?

Teachers and Teacher Training

One key factor is that many teachers simply have not been trained. One survey of primary school teachers in thirteen English-speaking African countries, for example, found that the percentage of unqualified teachers varied from a low of 19 per cent in Malawi to a high of 71 per cent in Liberia. The average figure for all thirteen was 42 per cent (Greenland, 1983: 7). In particular, those who find themselves teaching social studies have not had training in social studies education. This is a complaint that permeates ASSP literature and affects most affiliated countries (see e.g. ASSP, 1985).

In Uganda, for example, Odada attended a social studies seminar at a school with 157 teachers. Only 44 per cent of these teachers had seen the official social studies syllabus. All of the teachers stated that they had never been trained to teach social studies. At another social studies workshop for 60 teacher trainers, 75 per cent admitted complete ignorance about social studies. Even among a sample of thirty-two first-year students on a Diploma in Education course in 1985/6 who were to specialise in social studies, none had seen the social studies syllabus for primary or secondary schools. A further summary of twenty-six research reports on social studies education in Ugandan schools revealed very little relevant initial or in-service teacher training (Odada, 1988). Lack of effective and widespread in-service training (for both teachers and teacher-trainers) has also adversely affected the introduction of social studies in Kenya, as there is considerable evidence of lack of awareness of the content, aims and methods of social studies among those teachers supposed to be teaching it (see e.g. Mbugua, 1987).

Yet effective training is crucial, because there is considerable resistance among teachers to overcome. The traditional cultural patterns of the societies from which teachers come will seldom have encouraged the questioning of received wisdom or the practice of reflective enquiry (Obebe, 1985: 26). Teachers will also usually have experienced, both in their own schooling and in their teacher training, a traditional view of what constitutes 'knowledge'. In the humanities this will have been separate history and geography, rarely the social sciences and not integrated social studies. Therefore social studies does not have the status of 'real' knowledge in the eyes of many teachers.

Moreover the methods of learning experienced by many teachers are at variance with those necessary for critical education in social studies. Hawes puts this well in relation to science, but it applies equally to social studies:

> Consider the case of a teacher brought up in the hard school where right answers are rewarded by praise and wrong answers by the cane. Now he is being invited to learn along with the children in Science, to admit ignorance (he the headmaster!), to reward discovery learning when neither he nor the children know the answer. Small wonder that he seldom responds to the challenge. (1979: 97)

In situations where teachers are also often paid a meagre salary and face large classes with slender resources, it is not surprising that attitudes to the extra work involved in new methods of critical pedagogy are either negative or quietly resistant. For example, one survey of the attitudes of primary school teachers in Kenya to the new social studies course found that despite a semblance of acquiescence there was still a sense of reservation. The teachers did not see any need to stress skills that related to the affective domain; they saw this as a province outside their preserve (Ochieng-Moya, 1985: 71). Similar attitudes were also found in Nigeria (Obebe, 1980).

However, there are some indications that good teacher training can make a difference. Teachers in Lesotho felt that workshops provided by the social studies project had increased their understanding of the social studies approach and this would help to implement key aspects of it, such as more pupil participation (Rees, 1980). In Nigeria, it was found that where students in a teacher training college are taught by tutors who have attended several in-service courses they were better prepared in both content and methodology than those who were taught by tutors who had not attended such courses (Obebe, 1980).

The nature of teacher training courses is also very important. The ASSP stresses that teachers themselves must experience the enquiry approach in their own learning in order to be able to use the method in the classroom (Merryfield, 1986: 79). One Nigerian writer for instance, argues that 'the habits picked up in our teacher training days stay with us and form a considerable foundation for our behaviour in the classroom' (Dubey, 1980: 74). Another notes that 'The colleges are known to encourage students' dependence on their teachers through the predominant use of lecture notes and dictation methods' (Udofoot, 1988: 8). The use of more participant democratic and co-operative learning methods in social studies teacher training should help to facilitate the greater use of these in the classroom. This is further discussed in chapter 7.

Teacher attitudes and practices are also affected by the level of resource provision. More participant teaching methods, such as regular discussions, are also greatly facilitated by stimulus material, such as textbook extracts, audio-visual aids, games and stimulations, handouts/worksheets, etc. The World Bank has provided a stark description of the situation in Africa. Educational material accounts for just 1.1 per cent of the recurrent primary education budget in the median African country. This allocation amounts to less than $0.60 per pupil a year, which buys very little in the way of books, slates, wall charts and writing implements. Even the most ingenious teacher finds it hard to teach children very much (World Bank, 1988: 35).

In seventeen trial schools used to pilot a new primary social studies course in Lesotho, the average pupil-teacher ratio was 64: 1. Actual class sizes varied from 117 to 36. Of the seventeen schools, eleven had no writing paper, eight had no books, four had no chart paper, six had no card, nine had no pencils and fourteen had no library. The teachers themselves saw the main constraints to the new course as too many children and a lack of textbooks and other teaching materials (Rees, 1980: 3). Evidence on social studies teaching in other African countries (e.g. Zambia, Liberia, Uganda and Kenya) confirms that the shortage of teaching resources is a widespread problem (Chamba, 1974/5; Brown, 1985; Odada, 1988; Ochieng-Moya, 1985). Enterprising teachers can no doubt use their initiative to improve the situation by such tactics as greater use of the environment, using visitors, getting free material from local factories and making teaching aids themselves with the help of pupils (Hawes, 1979: 148–53). However, there is little doubt that shortages of teaching resources are a severe hindrance to the development of more active teaching methods in social studies in African schools.

Assessment

Assessment cannot be ignored in the school setting. If a subject is to be taken seriously by parents, pupils and teachers, then some form of public assessment is usually necessary. The key question, however, is what type of assessment.

Teachers tend to teach according to what they think will be assessed rather than their assessment being based on what they have decided to teach. Thus the nature of classroom teaching will be greatly influenced by the nature of public assessment. Unfortunately, assessment has often been in the form of timed examinations stressing factual recall:

> It is by no means surprising therefore, to find that the vast majority of items in Social Studies and Science papers demand straight recall of specific facts and that teaching is adjusted accordingly; in one paper analysed in Botswana out of fifty questions forty-nine required only factual recall of information. (Hawes, 1979: 103)

The question of assessment tends on the whole to be ignored in the ASSP and other material on social studies education that has been referred to in this chapter. Yet the type of critical social education desired by the ASSP will require the assessment of skills as well as knowledge. For example, this list of skills comes from the final year of primary social studies in The Gambia (1984);

1   To be able to listen, speak, read and write effectively and present an oral and written report.
2   Think constructively and ask sensible questions.
3   Discuss critically and accept constructive criticism.
4   Plan, direct and participate in group and community activities.
5   Read and make graphs, maps, charts and tables. Interpret and make simple models.

Measured attainment of objectives like these requires a diverse package of assessment techniques – for example, orals (individual and group), comprehension and analysis of statistical, written and verbal data, short essays and a profile or record of achievement (perhaps a mixture of self and tutor assessment) to cover group and community activities. The introduction of these assessment methods has major implications for both in-service teacher training and for resources in terms of teacher time and the provision of textbooks and other teaching material containing more stimulus data and questions for discussion.

Conclusion – The Future

If schools in Africa in the future are going to educate for democracy and human rights and against prejudice, bias, hostility and intolerance then the organisation of both classrooms and schools must be more congruent with these aims. Of course, schools in Africa face enormous difficulties in developing democratic education where it did not exist before but examining the principles and ideas underlying education for democracy in the African context is the beginning of the process of overcoming these difficulties.

In terms of classrooms this means that teaching methods across the curriculum must become more active, participant, co-operative, investigative and critical in order to develop democratic citizens. Yet most importantly of all, the curriculum will have to contain time for a direct and explicit examination of social and political issues and structures. This is because democracy is based on a notion of political choice but choice based on political ignorance is no choice at all.

Research by Osler (1993a) suggests that young people in Africa can be very well aware of this. Osler investigated the production and use in schools of a magazine on environmental and development education call *Pied Crow* in Kenya. When asked to give opinions on suitable topics for future editions of the magazine, pupils in every school she visited demanded more information on politics. They particularly requested material on democracy, on multi-partyism and on the next President of Kenya, and felt they needed to be helped in developing the skill of identifying bias.

What would the nature of such political education be? Essentially it must not only provide political knowledge and develop political skills, but it must also possess an underlying democratic ideology if it is to succeed. The major reason why civic education courses in schools in the past have had so little impact on pupils is the didactic, descriptive, passive and non-controversial nature of the course concerned (Stacey, 1978: 67–8). The exact nature of the democratic values to be encouraged may vary from society to society but the following two lists illustrate the common emphasis on freedom, justice, tolerance and human rights. The first is from the pro-gramme for Political Education devised in Britain during the 1970s:

- willingness to adopt a critical stance towards political information;

- willingness to give reasons why one holds a view or acts in a certain way;
- respect for evidence in forming and holding political opinions;
- willingness to open the possibility of changing one's own attitudes in the light of evidence;
- to value fairness as a criterion for judging and making decisions;
- to value the freedom to choose between political alternatives;
- toleration of a diversity of ideas, beliefs, values and interests. (Porter, 1979)

The second is from a study of education for citizenship in a multicultural society:

> Under attitudes, students should be enabled to develop a respect for persons, for reciprocity and justice in human relations and for the rule of law; a commitment to democratic processes, including the process of rational discourse and peaceful conflict resolution; a conviction of the core importance of human rights in human relations . . . an appreciation of their moral stewardship of their environment and natural resources; a commitment to social responsibility . . . (and to) moral autonomy in decision-making. (Lynch, 1992: 50)

However, this emphasis on toleration does not mean a completely laissez-faire, anything goes approach. There are certain values which are incompatible with open, democratic classroom political discussion based on equal human rights. Racism, for example, is not just another political issue because racist opinions assume that people are unequal on the irrelevant basis of skin colour and it therefore contradicts the idea of equality of opinion essential to democracy. Similarly sexist opinions assume inequality on the irrelevant basis of gender. Democratic political education can, and must, educate about racism and sexism but must also itself be anti-racist and anti-sexist. While this has obvious implications for education in those African countries such as Zimbabwe, Namibia and, in particular South Africa, which have recently been subject to white racist regimes, it also has lessons for most other African countries in terms of the tolerance of ethnic pluralism and encouragement of equal respect for all ethnic groups.

This may also mean altering the way in which school teaching materials deal with ethnicity. One study, for example, found that Kenyan school textbooks give a high profile to ethnicity and tribe. The ethnic group was portrayed as an important unit of activity. In a few instances descriptions of certain ethnic groups, especially the Maasai and other nomadic peoples, carried somewhat derogatory notions. Each ethnic group was portrayed as a cultural enclave, thus presenting a landscape of multiple 'islands' without structural linkages between them, though there were no references to ethnic rivalries. In Tanzania, on the other hand, there were far fewer references to ethnicity and textbooks focused more on the Tanzanian nation-state. When references to ethnicity occurred the stress was on the contribution of various ethnic cultural heritages to the common Tanzanian culture (Mbuyi, 1988). A combination of both approaches would seem preferable. It is important to be realistic and to openly recognise that ethnic and cultural diversity exists, but also to do so positively and tolerantly and to describe links between ethnic groups and the significance of the nation-state as well.

It is encouraging that there is evidence that more open, democratic classrooms making greater use of discussion and other participatory methods can foster a range of democratic political orientations, such as greater political interest, less authoritarianism, greater political knowledge and a greater sense of political efficacy (Ehman, 1980). Research in Israel demonstrated that different forms of classroom relationship facilitate or impede the development of pupils' political efficacy and orientation to public forms of political involvement (Ichilov, 1991). Significantly, democratic and co-operative teaching methods have also been shown to reduce inter-ethnic conflict and to promote cross-cultural friendship (Lynch, 1992: 22). A recent study of ethnically mixed schools in the south-eastern United States compared two schools that stressed co-operative learning, the development of interpersonal relationships, values clarification and the heterogeneous grouping of students with three traditional schools where students were streamed by achievement and taught in a lecture-recitation style in predominantly same-race classes. The study found that cross-race interaction and friendships and a positive evaluation of different race students were significantly higher in the former than the latter schools (Conway and Damico, 1993).

There are also some encouraging signs that, despite the educational problems and constraints discussed above, attention is now being paid to the creation of more democratic classrooms in Africa. In West Africa there are clear indications of a renewed interest in human rights education, with programmes in junior secondary schools in Ghana and Nigeria. The defeat of the dictatorial Mengistu regime in Ethiopia in 1991 and moves towards democratic government have meant that human rights education is seen as a curriculum priority and is regarded by the Minister of Education as the basis upon which to build education for a democratic state (Osler, 1993b). Namibia, South Africa and Eritrea are three case studies of attempts to introduce more democratic classrooms and these are discussed in more detail in the final chapters of this book.

6

Democratic Management and School Effectiveness in Africa: Learning from Tanzania

In February 1967 at Arusha in northern Tanzania the then President, Julius Nyerere, announced that Tanzania would follow the path of African socialism. In the same year Nyerere, who had himself been a teacher, also published *Education for Self Reliance* (ESR) which was both a critique of the colonial education system inherited by Tanzania and a set of educational policies for producing schools and citizens more in tune with African socialism. These policies included, among others, the idea that primary schooling would be a complete educational stage in itself and not just a preparation for secondary education; that each school would also be a productive enterprise with students gaining experience of, and respect for, manual labour; that classroom theory would be integrated with practical experience in the productive enterprise; that schools would have closer links with the community; that political education would be compulsory; and that character assessment would be introduced alongside academic assessment.

In the twenty-five years since its introduction a number of studies evaluating the shortcomings and achievements of the various features of ESR have been published (Saunders, 1982; Cooksey, 1986; Harber, 1989: ch. 4; Hinzen and Hunsdorfer, 1979; Mosha, 1990). However, one key aspect of ESR, the democratic organisation of secondary schools, has received relatively little attention in the literature on Tanzania, especially in terms of empirical research. This chapter considers the experience of Tanzania in relation to democratic schools in the context of the debates surrounding 'effective schooling'. However, it must be noted that schools in Africa, especially outside the capital city, often operate in conditions of severe financial stringency and consequently face shortages of trained staff, teaching materials and other educational resources of all kinds. Such schools often cannot achieve the basic criteria for school effectiveness listed in European and American books on the subject. Hence it is probably more accurate to ask whether participatory forms of school management can help to decrease school ineffectiveness rather than increase effectiveness.

Democratic Schools as Government Policy

One prominent Tanzanian educationalist has noted that:

> The primary objective of the Arusha Declaration was to build a state guided by fundamental principles of equality, respect for human dignity, democracy, work by all and exploitation by none. (Mosha, 1990: 60)

Democracy was therefore supposed to be at the forefront of the Tanzanian version of African socialism from the outset. It can, of course, be argued that the top-down decision to opt for socialism and the existence of a one-party state (albeit one that allowed for electoral competition between party members) have limited democracy in practice. Nevertheless, within these parameters Nyerere was convinced of the need for democratic debate in the interpretation and implementation of African socialism. In *Education for Self Reliance* he argued strongly that pupils must be involved in making decisions about the school-based productive enterprises as 'only then can the participants practise – and learn to value – direct democracy . . . the pupils must be able to participate in decisions and learn by mistakes' (Nyerere, 1967: 28–9). So one cardinal objective of ESR was to:

> promote a sense of belonging together and enhance the spirit of co-operation by making pupils value work, practise their democratic rights, but also become accountable in their responsibilities. (Mosha, 1990: 60)

This objective rapidly became policy as a directive from the Chief Education Officer in May 1968 regarding secondary schools made clear:

> So as to involve the whole school there should be a committee comprising of staff and pupils, chaired by the headteacher, with the agriculture teacher acting as secretary. Where the headteacher is also the agriculture teacher, then another teacher should be appointed secretary. The pupils should be represented in the committee either in classes or houses. All planning and preparation of projects should be done in the committee and each project such as chicken keeping,

vegetable gardening etc. should have a pupil as the secretary keeping the records. (Mwingira, 1968)

Tanzania was therefore one of the first countries to insist at the official level on pupil participation and representation through such committees. Even now support for more democratic school structures at the national policy-making level is unusual, even in those European countries that term themselves democracies, though Denmark, for example, is an honourable exception (Harber and Meighan, 1989; Jensen and Walker, 1989). In Africa, Mozambique seems to be one of the few other countries that have tried to democratise schools on a system-wide basis (Searle,1981).

The key organ for the operation of democracy in Tanzanian secondary schools is the school council. The National Policy on School Councils (Ministry of Education, 1979) spells out what the composition of a school council at a secondary school should be:

1   The Chairperson will be the Chairperson of the Party (Chama Cha Mapinduzi) Youth League at the school and will simultaneously be the head prefect of the school. Therefore s/he is elected by the whole student body and by the CCM Youth League members at the school.
2   The Secretary is elected by the vote of the whole school council.
3   Members of the council. One pupil representative from each class stream and two from each dormitory in a boarding school. In a day school, one representative for every fifty pupils. Teachers vote for one representative for every fifteen teachers.
4   Headteacher Appointees. The headteacher appoints two pupils, one non-teaching staff and one teacher to the council.
5   Ex-officio members. These have no right to vote. They include the deputy head of the school who is consultant/adviser for the council; the school bursar; the head cook; the Chairperson and Secretary of the CCM branch at the school and the Secretary of the CCM youth branch at the school.
6   The council should also have the following committees: the executive committee; a disciplinary committee; an economic committee; a committee for culture, sports and games; a committee for education and politics; a committee for health; a food committee.

The National Policy on School Councils also says that the school council should meet at least once in two months and its executive committee once a month. It lists the functions of the council as follows:

1   To aid the government so as to educate the students on government policy, especially in regard to implementation.

2   To be the advisory body to the headteacher on student matters, plans and implementation.
3   To be the centre for learning leadership among the students in developing the school.
4   To arouse the students' interest in decision making.
5   To build and intensify cooperation and good relationships among the teachers, students and non-teaching workers of the school.
6   To look after student discipline.
7   To discuss and give suggestions on the school regulations.
8   To make sure that the school regulations are honoured and followed.
9   To arrange the duties and powers of the student leaders.
10 To keep an eye on the income and expenditure of the money obtained from all ESR activities.

However, the extent to which councils really exist in schools and the way in which they actually function is open to question. Among a sample of twenty-one headteachers, for example, who were asked what was the most important aspect of self-reliance in their school, none specified democratic participation. When asked more specifically what were the most important changes in teachers' practices prompted by the implementation of self-reliance, only four said that it had allowed students to participate in decision making (Saunders, 1982). Headteachers in government schools have differed with respect to the extent to which they have welcomed democratic practices in the schools. Indeed, Mbilinyi et al. have recently argued that the majority of schools are still authoritarian and reinforce passive subordination among students (1991: 59), even in those schools where councils do function as outlined above:

> Ultimately, of course, such councils still mask the reality, which is that the Headmaster or Headmistress has ultimate authority in the school, so that he/she has the option of ignoring student ideas or opposing them. (Mbilinyi, 1979: 105)

Thus, as Kisanga (1986) suggests, the present position in school councils in Tanzania from the pupils' point of view is perhaps most accurately characterised as consultative participation rather than direct democracy as, although pupils are able to discuss and influence school policy, the headteacher retains the final veto.

The Case for Greater Democratisation

Nevertheless, pupils in many schools in Tanzania still expect to have an influence over school policy and are expected to do so by the staff. While the final say may remain with the head, this attempt to institutionalise a consultative-democratic situation is still significantly different from the bureaucratic-authoritarian nature of school organisation in most of Africa and elsewhere (Harber, 1991 and 1992).

One of the key arguments for organising schools more democratically (and the one used by Nyerere above) concerns an issue often played down or glossed over in the literature on school effectiveness – the question of effective at what? There is an enormous variety of possible goals and priorities in education but the conventional literature on school effectiveness tends to focus on immediate and easily measurable indicators of effectiveness such as exam results and truancy rates, and as a consequence other important aims tend to be neglected. Yet it only really makes sense to think of effectiveness in terms of what a school is actually trying to achieve and if a key aim of education in a democratic state should be the creation of democratic citizens then this ought be reflected in school organisation and ethos. The argument that democratic values and behaviour are best learned by experience of democracy in practice was well summed up by the British Schools Council in The Practical Curriculum:

> Some values, like those of democracy, tolerance and responsibility, grow only with experience of them. Social education arises from a school's ethos, its organisation and its relation with the community. The way a school organises its staff and pupils and its formal rules, say a great deal about its real values and attitudes. Schools need to practice what they seek to promote. (1981)

Moreover, research evidence from the United States and Britain (Hepburn, 1984; John and Osborne, 1992) does indeed suggest that more democratic school structures can foster democratic values and skills among young people. It may be that in Tanzania at present this form of political education has more potential than the formal curriculum provision of a subject called political education ('siasa') as the evidence suggests that this has tended to be poorly resourced and badly taught by untrained teachers (Harber, 1989: ch. 4).

However, even in terms of the more conventional aims of schooling such as better exam results there are four main arguments that greater democracy and participation in school management can help to make schools more effective (or less ineffective).

1   Rules are better kept by staff and pupils if democratically agreed to in the first place.

2   Communications in the school are improved.
3   There is an increased sense of responsibility as staff and pupils have more control over their own organisation.
4   Decision making is improved as a range of internal and external interests and opinions is considered.

Empirical studies of school effectiveness in Europe and America have, in fact, found that effective school management is related to staff having a sense of control over the school programme and worthwhile and efficient inter-departmental meetings and planning exercises. This sense of involvement and influence in the institution is also true of pupils. A favourable school climate has been linked with students sensing that the school as a social system is not a meaningless environment in which they can exert little control over what happens to them (Reid, Hopkins and Holly, 1987). Rutter (1979), in his research on school effectiveness, concluded that schools that give a large proportion of pupils responsibility – either in terms of caring for their own resources, participating in meetings or holding some kind of post – had better exam results, better behaviour and attendance, and less delinquency. Can school councils, therefore, assist school effectiveness in a developing country like Tanzania?

School Councils in Tanzania

The following account of the operation of two school councils in Tanzania is best described in Walker's (1974) phrase as 'condensed field work'. This is a qualitative study of shorter duration than an ethnography, relying principally on interviews, the collection of documents and short periods of observation. This was carried out over a period of two and a half weeks in April 1992 and involved interviews and the collection of documentation in the Ministry of Education, Dar Es Salaam and in two secondary schools. School A is located about 35 kilometres outside Dar Es Salaam while school B (an all girls school) is near to Moshi in northern Tanzania. As suggested in the earlier part of this chapter, schools in Tanzania vary in the extent to which they have actually implemented the policy of having a school council. These two schools were chosen after discussion with Ministry of Education officials because they were known to have a functioning school council. The aim of the research was to see what was possible, i.e. what a 'successful' school council looked like in Tanzania and how pupils and teachers reacted to it. Therefore, apart from the collection of documentation pertaining to the school councils (constitutions, records of meetings etc.), interviews were also carried out with the headteacher, three other teachers and two senior pupils at school A and two teachers and two senior pupils at school B.

School A

The structure of the School Council at school A is similar, though not identical to, the national guidelines for school councils outlined above. Each house elects four 'MPs' and each stream or year group elects two MPs. The head then has the power to appoint up to five members of the school community and seven teachers. Other members currently include the chair and secretary of the CCM branch (though this may have to change with the move to multi-party democracy) and eight prefects, including the head prefect, dormitory prefect, dining hall, library and health prefects. (Some prefects are elected and some appointed by the head-teacher.) The chair, vice-chair, secretary and deputy secretary of the council are all elected by the other members of the council.

A key objective of the school council is 'to propose and agree upon the school rules for the benefit of the school community' and to see that they are put into effect. The council apparatus for doing this consists of the general assembly (i.e. everybody on the council) and a number of functional sub-committees which cover food and the dining hall; self-reliance activities; games; culture and recreation; discipline; education and the library; cleanliness and maintenance. There is also an executive committee consisting of the chair of the full school council, the vice-chair, the secretary and the chairs of the different sub-committees. This acts as a sort of cabinet co-ordinating the work of the sub-committees and drawing up the agenda of the general assembly based on the proposals stemming from the sub-committees. Elected pupils and relevant staff sit on all of the functional sub-committees.

If this is the formal apparatus of the council, how does it carry out its work and what is its relationship with the headteacher? This is perhaps best explored by looking at examples of issues raised through the sub-committees. The self-reliance committee, for example, manages all the different productive enterprises associated with the school.(Under the policy of ESR introduced by Nyerere each school is supposed to manage productive agricultural enterprises on which the pupils work and the proceeds of which help in the maintenance of the school.) This means that it supervises the budgets of the school's various projects (e.g. a piggery, orange fields and the school shop) and has to report to the general assembly on the state of the accounts every six months. It also makes proposals on the expenditure of receipts from the projects.

If this is for a small amount, e.g. to buy some seeds, then it takes the decision itself. However, if the proposal is to spend a larger amount of the money generated by ESR projects as, for example, in the case of a recent graduation ceremony, then it has to go to the general assembly. When large sums of money are being discussed the headteacher chairs the committee. When asked what would happen if the student members wanted to spend money on something and the headteacher did not, it was suggested that the head would have the final say but that there had not been a fundamental disagreement in thirteen years. The head knew beforehand what was coming up and there was always a negotiated agreement.

One pupil on the ESR committee also provided recent examples of how it both influenced decision making and ensured that rules are carried out. As part of ESR the pupils used to cultivate plots (preparing the ground, weeding etc.) but watering was in the hands of paid workmen. However, it became clear through complaints from pupils to the ESR committee that the crops were not as successful as they should be because the workmen were not reliable. The pupils therefore decided to do everything themselves rather than lose the produce, and the workmen were out of a job. In its policy implementation role, the committee had recently discovered that some pupils who were supposed to be taking rubbish from the school to a nearby rubbish pit were not doing so and it ensured that they would do so in the future.

Another committee is the disciplinary committee or rather committees, as there are two, one with students only and one with students and staff. If it is a minor offence then the student committee can allocate minor punishments such as grass cutting or cleaning (despite the inconsistency of using work as a punishment in an educational system that is supposed to encourage a respect for manual labour). If, however, it is a more serious offence then it will go to the joint committee who will make a recommendation to the headteacher. For example, in March 1991 some students left the school at night to go to a disco. The committee recommended to the head that the pupils be suspended but instead the head decided that the pupils be caned and made to do some hard physical work around the school premises. While caning was obviously regarded as a less serious punishment than suspension or expulsion it nevertheless has actually been legally banned in Tanzania. Moreover, it does, as one Tanzanian writer has argued (Mbilinyi, 1979: 104), sit oddly with school democracy, being more symbolic of the relationship between oppressor and oppressed than the desired relationship between co-operating individuals. It is also another example of the persistence of traditional, long-established cultural practices in the face of determined curriculum innovation from the centre. However, according to the pupils interviewed, it was used very infrequently in this school whereas in many other Tanzanian schools it is used on a regular basis (Mbilinyi et al., 1991: 59).

A final example is the work of the education committee which has as its main purposes reporting on academic problems in the school and suggesting strategies for academic improvement. Some years ago the school results were considered too low and a major factor in this was the existence of a teacher shortage. The committee therefore proposed, and got implemented, a system of peer tutoring based on study groups in which the students helped each other and also encouraged and persuaded older students to help with teaching lower down the school. The committee also proposed and organised help for weaker students outside normal classes. Very recently the committee had successfully proposed an debating club where all debates are in English in order to help to combat the decline in the standard of English among pupils that has occurred throughout Tanzania.

Sub-committees make their proposals to the general assembly of the school council. Interviewees were a little vague about how often this body meets but the average seemed to be between two and four times a term. Unanimous decisions can be negotiated, for example, in relation to the need for a crash programme for working in the shambas (ESR fields) in order to harvest the crops. On other matters where there is no agreement the assembly has to vote as it did so recently on a decision to have meat on Sundays rather than on Thursdays. Sometimes, however, there is disagreement but the decision cannot be settled by a vote, e.g. if pupils are coming from another school for games and nobody wants to give up their dormitory for the guests. Under such circumstances a negotiated settlement has to be argued out until a compromise arrangement is reached.

From the general assembly all decisions go to the headteacher who has the final say. Much of the time there appears to be agreement, as policy proposals are well informed in that they come out of the needs and experiences of the pupils. However, according to the pupils, when there is a real disagreement between the assembly and the headteacher that cannot be settled by negotiation, the headteacher gets his way not by openly saying 'no' but by the time honoured tactic of delay and not doing anything so that other issues emerge and take over the agenda.

Despite this final limit to the powers of the school council, which means that it it is advisory rather than decision making, it is clearly an influential body. All interviewees were definite that the advantages outweighed the disadvantages. Some of the advantages noted by the interviewees were as follows:

1   The council enables problems to be discussed before they get out of hand. In this way it improves communication and increases understanding and therefore, as the headteacher put it, avoids strikes. The pupils supported this and used the example of how they had recently got the use of Saturdays changed from working in the fields to individual academic work unless a crash programme such as harvesting was needed.

2   It is a good way of pre-testing or piloting a new policy. The Second Master used the recent example of when the school management proposed changing the school uniform to long trousers. This was put to the school council after discussion in the dormitories but was rejected by the majority of pupils because the of extra expense involved.

3   It reduces the workload on teachers as they are helped, especially in their non-teaching functions, by the pupils.

4   Discipline problems are reduced because, as the discipline master put it, 'staff are closer to students'.

5   It provides quite a number of pupils with experience of leadership and increases confidence and discussion skills generally.

The main disadvantage noted, especially by the teachers, was that it was time consuming. It was also pointed out that it did not work perfectly all the time, that occasionally there were still communication problems and sometimes the election of unsuitable representatives caused problems. However, the balance of the argument was summed up by one teacher who had been working in secondary schools in the twenty-five years since the Arusha declaration when he said that at first there was considerable mistrust and hostility among teachers but now he felt that teachers would be unhappy if councils did not exist.

School B

At school B the structure of the council differs from the national guidelines and has similarities with a national parliamentary system. The president is elected by all the pupils at the school after nominations from the pupils, which usually produce four or five candidates. At this stage the staff vet a little on the grounds of health and to make sure that whoever is chosen will not lose out academically as the post will make many demands on the winner's time. The successful candidate then chooses eight 'ministers' – education, finance, home affairs, health and social welfare, sports and culture, environment, agriculture and foreign affairs. These are again vetted by staff but it is very unusual for anybody to be rejected. The candidate for president with the second largest vote becomes vice-president. The President is usually from the fifth form and all ministers are from either the third form or the fifth form, as the fourth form and the sixth form are preparing for important examinations. Like national politicians, each minister is responsible for making proposals and monitoring developments in her area while the president and vice-president co-ordinate their activities in the manner of a prime minister.

Each separate class elects a class leader (eighteen in all) and each form elects a form coordinator (so six in all). There are also seven houses in the school which look after the dormitories and these each elect a leader. A secretary to the parliament to keep minutes of parliamentary and cabinet meetings is appointed by the president. All the above pupils plus one advisory member of staff goes to make up the school parliament (forty three in all). The constitution notes that 'The teacher adviser has got no right of voting but is there to advise only if it is necessary. She is an observer.' The school parliament meets weekly, cabinet meetings twice a month, class meetings weekly and house meetings once a month.

What can the cabinet and parliament make decisions about? One of the major tasks in any academic year is to plan the Programme of Activities. This includes a long list of duty rotas, inter- and intra-school sports and other competitions, outings, dances, plays and other cultural events, all of which are planned and executed by the pupils themselves. It is the responsibiliy of individual ministers to make sure that a planned event or duty in her field is actually carried out. At the end of the very full 1992 programme of events the headteacher has underlined the self-reliance nature of the undertaking by simply writing 'It can be done if you you play your part'.

This particular school has been very successful in selling the products from its self-reliance activities and in any one year there is roughly two million Tanzanian shillings (£4,500) in the self-reliance fund. The school council has power over this money and uses it to support the programme of activities or one-off, more expensive occasions such as parents' day. The headteacher will advise on this expenditure, if asked; but this is very rare.

However, perhaps a better feel of how the system at this school works and what is discussed is provided by the minutes from the different types of meetings. The following are extracts from the minutes of a class meeting, a cabinet meeting and a parliament meeting all held during 1991.

Class Meeting (Form 3)

1   One member suggested that letters concerning loans should be attached to the students' progress report so as to inform parents of the amount of money their daughters had to pay back. The class teacher informed the meeting that these letters are already supposed to be attached to the reports so perhaps the previous class teacher had forgotten to attach them. The teacher promised to give loan letters to those who did not receive them so that they could go to their parents.

2   Another member pointed out that the form three shamba dresses (for working in the self-reliance fields) were worn out and too small. She requested that new dresses be made. The class teacher said the tailor would come on the 14th to take measurements for the new dresses.

3   One member suggested that they should be provided with mattresses and exercise books earlier because parents do not buy these for the students yet they are listed in the letters of loans and are very important. The class teacher said that they are working hard to solve the problem.

Cabinet Meeting

Minister for Environment – said that form 1 should trim the flowers and cut the edges of flower beds ready for parents day.

Minister for Finance – said that all those students who are going to participate in the hairstyle show on parents day and needed a rasta hairstyle should give her the money so that she could organise it.

Speaker – Thursday will be the last day for washing, the laundry will be closed after that.

Minister for Sports and Culture – said that the singing and glee club will be checked on the song for the hairstyle show on Thursday. She also announced the arrangements for the staff and students annual dinner, listing what each year would do on the occasion.

Student Leader – said that all leaving houseleaders should collect all cleaning tools and hand them to the new houseleaders.

Parliament Meeting

A representative from form 3 thanked the sixth form for invigilating their exams. She also asked if they could plait their hair when going home.

A representative from the school's catholics thanked the school for giving their choir the chance to lead at a former teacher's wedding mass.

A representative from form five suggested it would be safer if the laboratories and dormitories facing the fence could have lights outside.

The Minister for Education told the class-leaders of forms four and three to clean their windows and that all broken lockers, windows and lost keys should be paid for.

The vice-student leader informed members that the general prayer would be held at 10.00 a.m. at the assembly ground and that students shouldn't sleep or talk during the prayer.

The student leader reminded the parliament of the correct steps for raising an issue. She said that one student had told the headmistress that there were bees at the infirmary but that this should have been reported to the Minister for Health and then brought to the cabinet if necessary.

When asked about the advantages of organising a school in this manner the teachers and pupils mentioned the following:

1   It trains the pupils to be self-disciplined, responsible and self-reliant. It becomes routine to look after yourself and keep the school clean and well organised.
2   The school works more smoothly – 'we live like a family', 'you learn to solve problems by discussion'.
3   It eases the work of the teacher and allows them to concentrate more on the academic development of the pupils.
4   It improves communication – 'there are no secrets'; 'we have no riots because pressure does not build' as the staff put it or, as one of the pupils who had been to another school said, 'They don't just ignore you here and tell you to go away'.
5   Those who take leadership roles in the school often go on to become quite prominent.
6   The pupils become very creative, e.g. a visitor is coming at very short notice and they will organise an excellent reception because they know each others' talents.
7   There is a friendlier relationship all round. Many activities, e.g. dances, involve both staff and students – 'This is the first school I have worked in where the pupils are proud of their teachers. It is very different from elsewhere.'

Neither staff nor pupils, despite being pressed by the interviewer, could think of any disadvantages in this particular school.

Participation and Violence in African Schools

In School A one interviewee argued that the presence of a school council had avoided strikes and another in School B argued that it avoided riots. Such findings may help to alleviate a problem that contributes to ineffectiveness in secondary schools in Africa, that of violent riots and demonstrations by pupils. There are regular accounts of these in the African press and examples from Nigeria, Kenya and Tanzania are described in Harber (1989: 124–6). The root cause of the problem is that schools in Africa are often authoritarian institutions in which pupils are socialised to depend on the authority structure of the school. However, at the same time pupils are very anxious about their success as families can have spent considerable amounts of money on their education and will have high expectations of them. Yet because of resource problems, poor communications and untrained staff, things often go wrong – food is in short supply, classes are left untaught, examination papers fail to appear on time. The system the pupils depend on and which is important to their future fails them. No explanation is forthcoming because there is no regular system of explanation and no expectation that the headteacher should explain what has happened. Indeed, complaints are often met with high handed authoritarianism. These two examples from the Kenyan press were published as the writer was on his way to, and then coming back from, doing the research in Tanzania described above:

> Parents of the Kamiru Boys' High School on Thursday went to the school and took away their children, leaving the institution deserted. Several parents told the *Sunday Nation* that they took the drastic step after disagreeing with the head-master over a number of issues, They accused the headmaster of being arrogant. They claimed that he had refused to tell them about their children's academic progress. They said that when a parent goes to the school to ask what his or her child's progress or mistakes are, they are told to go home with the child. (*Sunday Nation*, 5 April 1992)

> Parents at Malava Secondary School yesterday criticised its management for failing to diffuse student unrest and urged the authorities to order the immediate reopening of the institution. The parents accused the headmaster of allegedly misleading the board of governors into approving the school's indefinite closure without proper investigations. They contended that if the headmaster had accepted to talk with the

students, the tension would have been diffused. (*Kenya Times*, 26 March 1992)

This authoritarianism and lack of communication leads to misunderstanding and suspicion, and resentment grows until a small incident can spark off serious and violent disturbances. Indeed, what might seem a relatively trivial to a teacher, such as whether or not milk is provided at breakfast or whether to wear long or short trousers (issues that have caused trouble in schools in Nigeria and Tanzania), can be very significant to pupils and in an existing context of malaise and frustration can be the trigger for violent disorder. Thus decision making procedures in schools need to enable pupils to make their viewpoint heard. One headteacher in Dadey's study of Ghana, for example, observed that:

> In this country, misinformation is the major cause of school disturbances. I regularly explain school policies to staff and students. This is a responsibility I do not delegate if I am in the school.

Another headteacher listed what he thought were the major causes of pupil disturbances in Ghana. The first four were all about communication, dialogue and lack of participation:

- absence or slowness of information flow
- breakdown in communications
- headteacher keeping students at arm's length
- lack of interest in students' welfare matters

He also listed the ways in which he had attempted to develop communication links with pupils:

1   Formal meetings – school durbars at which all students are present; student council meetings in which each form is represented on the council; committee meetings, e.g. food committee, entertainment committee.
2   Informal meetings – on the school compound; at the head's office or residence.
3   Regular reports from student leaders – weekly report from the senior prefect; weekly report from the dining hall prefect (*Dadey*, 1990: 80, 316–18).

Conclusion

Staff and pupils in the two Tanzanian schools described above were clear that the benefits of a more democratic school structure outweighed any disadvantages. Although the context and problems differ, this matches findings from Europe and America that more participant organisation increases school effectiveness as well as enhancing democratic values and skills. Comments from the staff and pupils at these two schools also suggest that it improves communication and helps to produce less authoritarian and more friendly day-to-day relationships than exist in many other schools in Tanzania and elsewhere in Africa. It may well therefore not only be a way of mitigating some of the difficulties of school management in a context of severe stringency but it might also be a way of avoiding the risk of violent disturbances in secondary schools that staff and pupils in Tanzania seemed all too well aware of. What would be useful now in further exploring these issues would be a fuller and more detailed ethnographic study using participant observation to examine the day-to-day realities of a democratic school in Tanzania in the same way that Gordon (1986) did with a democratic school in Britain.

7

Teacher Education and Political Development

As was argued in chapter 4, schools in Africa are currently predominantly authoritarian-bureaucratic institutions with teacher–student relationships in the classroom reflecting this authoritarian environment and being based on Freire's 'banking' theory of knowledge which is characterised by exposition and rote learning. One factor helping to perpetuate this situation is the role of teacher education by failing to break the cycle of authoritarian schools – authoritarian teacher training – authoritarian teachers – authoritarian schools.

This is important as genuine education for democracy will require a substantial change in the nature of the relationship between teachers and students. If a central concern of education is not only to be learning about human rights and democratic political institutions but also learning democratic values, then classroom ethos or atmosphere will have to change not only in those lessons devoted to civic or political education but also right across the curriculum and in the everyday life of the schools. Changing the processes of schooling is as important as changing the content. This means classrooms characterised by greater participation and emphasising procedural values such as tolerance, mutual respect and freedom of expression. In such classrooms students possess rights – to be listened to, to be respected and to be treated fairly – and have the duty to observe the rights of others. Students in such classrooms are also not treated simply as empty vessels to be filled up but have the right to at least some say in determining what they learn and how. Achieving this type of classroom will require major changes in the nature and processes of teacher education to make it more consistent with what is desired in the classroom.

Contradictions in Teacher Education

An important argument concerning the contradictions in teacher education is that of the 'myth of the liberal college' (Bartholemew, 1978). This attacks the myth that there is any real difference between the 'liberal and progressive' teacher training colleges on the one hand and the traditional and conservative schools on the other. Rather than there being a contradiction between the two over what is taught and learned, how and when, the former is in fact an authoritarian preparation for the latter. It is not a case of student teachers forgetting what they have learned at college once they enter the 'real world' of schools but rather that the relationships between students and tutors in college or university has actually prepared them for it.

One reason for this is the contradiction between 'do as I say' rather than 'do as I do'. Tutors may well talk about the use of participant and enquiry-based classroom methods but rarely use them themselves. In a study of a teacher education college in Uganda, for example, it was found that the students said that they most frequently experienced didactic methods and much less frequently experienced participant ones, whereas the tutors in the college gave the opposite answer. In particular, students said that they experienced a great deal of note dictation whereas the tutors said that this was one of the methods most infrequently used. However, both groups tended to blame this on large classes, a lack of teaching materials and an over-burdened curriculum. The writer concluded that:

> Teacher training in Uganda with its emphasis on formal learning and experience in schools seems to be preparing student-teachers for Uganda 'as it is' rather than changing it, for example, in the direction desired by President Museveni and the NRM. The government's targeted goal is to build an independent, integrated, self-sustaining national economy and this will require independent, flexible and self-sufficient citizens. (Rugamba, 1990: 62–3)

A detailed study of teacher education in Botswana (Mannathoko 1995) discovered a similar situation. Students complained that time and again lecturers told them to use child-centred methods when teaching in schools when the lecturers themselves did not use the methods when teaching them. As one student at a teacher training college said:

> We think that lecturers should demonstrate the variety of teaching methods they say we should use in school classrooms by practising those methods here when teaching us. (p. 317)

Students provided examples of lecturers who adhered to the lecture method as a matter of principle even when inappropriate because lecturing was the one method that epitomised the intellectual status of a tertiary institution. The lecturers claimed that it was the business of the students to listen and to take their own notes because 'it was not the business of the lecturer to spoon-feed them'. Yet by relying primarily on this method spoon-feeding was exactly what was happening.

This study also found another interesting contradiction relevant to education for democracy, which is almost certainly not unique to Botswana. At the university there exists an institution-wide gender equality policy. Yet both male and female lecturers accepted that it was 'normal' for female school and university teacher education students to be shy, passive and obedient whereas male students are assertive, noisy and inquisitive (Mannathoko, 1995: 322–3).

A study of teacher education in Zimbabwe (Nagel, 1992) also found considerable evidence of the myth of the liberal college. Teaching in the colleges of education was overwhelmingly lecturer-centred and authoritarian with regular examples of dictation of notes word for word, and with lecturers giving students marks for such note-taking. As a result there was little difference between the schools and teacher education with the latter failing to change ideas about education inherited by the student teachers from their own school experience:

> The students in teacher colleges have recently come out of the schools where they have spent eleven years of their lives. Half of the 480 student teacher respondents I asked had previously also been working as untrained teachers. They carry with them images and ideas from this experience of what schooling should be like. Finally, a close relationship between basic education and teacher education is upheld also in teaching practice, where the Zimbabwean students spend one whole year working as full-time teachers. By and large this assumption that teacher education reproduces current ideas and practices that are found in schools does not seem to be exaggerated. (Nagel, 1992: 20)

Moreover, both schools and teacher education colleges reflected a traditional culture which does not encourage questioning in general, by children in particular and by female children at all. So that student teachers said that they would rather not pose questions in class. When the writer asked students if they would like to suggest other ways of doing things in class they looked terrified and said that they would never dream of suggesting anything to their lecturers, let alone comment upon their teaching. Nagel notes the resulting contradiction:

> In colleges of teacher education, modern theories of child upbringing are taught. These are often treated verbatim and in a seemingly meaningless manner in students' assignments. One of the reasons for this is that they are literally meaningless to the students, in a very literal sense, as they coincide with few of the students' own

experiences. How could they possibly come to understand a pedagogy which is really child-centred, as they claim it to be these days,
unless the teaching of this concept takes their own experiences into
consideration? It is through dialogue about the 'taken-for-granted', the
implicit meanings, the new beliefs and practices can become conscious
knowledge and serve as a basis for professional reflection. Traditional
values, according to their nature, are usually not subjected to critical
discourse. (1992: 68)

Models of Teacher Education

Avalos (1991) has usefully identified a number of models of teacher
education. She argues that the dominant model in developing countries is what she terms the 'behavioural' model associated with such
approaches as 'competency-based teacher education' and 'mastery
learning'. In Botswana, for example, the textbooks used in teacher
education are strongly influenced by this model and the proceedings of
teacher education conferences are replete with lecturers' subscription
to it (Mannathoko, 1995: 320). The purpose of this model is to train
teachers who above all are skilled and competent performers and
therefore it stresses teaching skills and behavioural objectives for
student teachers as most important. The emphasis is on learning to
do rather than to think.

Despite its prevalence both in the West and in developing countries this model has attracted increasing criticism for its emphasis
on teacher 'training' as opposed to teacher 'education' (Popkewitz,
1987; Ginsberg, 1988). The main thrust of this criticism has been
that, while practical training in classroom teaching skills are obviously a vital element of learning to be a teacher, the behavioural
approach sees teaching only as a neutral, technical and politically
unproblematic act and ignores the wider social, political and economic context in which schools exist and classroom learning takes
place:

> Student teachers are generally introduced to a one-dimensional concep-
> tion of schooling . . . Schools as public sites are presented as if free of all
> vestiges of contestation, struggle and cultural politics. Classroom reality
> is rarely presented as socially constructed, historically determined and
> mediated through institutionalised relationships of class gender, race
> and power. (Popkewitz, 1987: 5)

Consequently teachers are seen as technicians robotically performing
mechanical tasks in the classroom or as though they were performing animals learning new tricks. Moreover, the teaching skills and
competencies that student teachers learn are overwhelmingly the

existing teacher-centred ones resulting in conformity to the status quo and reproduction of authoritarian schools and classrooms.

However, Al-Salmi (1994), reflecting on the situation in Oman and elsewhere in the Middle East, argues that there is another very common model in developing countries, but not one discussed by Avalos – the transmission model. In this model even practical teaching skills tend to get ignored and instead the emphasis is on book learning and the passing down of received wisdom about education from lecturers to students. The aim is to reproduce such knowledge uncritically but accurately in essays and examinations. Independent learning and group discussion are discouraged.

This model is also not absent in teacher education in Africa. Nagel (1992) portrays teacher education in Zimbabwe as being very influenced by this model. At one point, for example, he notes how the student teachers were obsessed with accurate note-taking in lectures. Moreover, they had to pay fines for not attending lectures which, he comments, 'was a measure of discipline [which] reflected very little pedagogical insight and was very typical of a repressive system' (p. 160).

These two models of teacher training can be contrasted with what Avalos terms the 'heuristic' and 'interactive' models. There is considerable overlap between these two models and, like Avalos herself, they will be described here as one heuristic/interactive model. The purpose of this model is to train teachers who are able to exercise reasoned judgement about goals to be achieved and appropriate alternative teaching methods. The procedures of training are participatory: there is a focus on reflective teaching and learning and hence students learn to question education as a social institution. Particularly within the interactive approach there is an emphasis on decision making based on trainer–trainee agreement on content and learning methods. In this model it would be truer to talk of teacher education rather than teacher training.

It is to this model that teacher education in Africa and elsewhere must look in the future if it is to prepare teachers who are better equipped for democratic education in schools. If teachers are going to teach in a more participant and democratic manner in schools, then the processes of their own education must be congruent with these methods. Linda Dove in her book *Teachers and Teacher Education in Developing Countries*, argues for such courses at both initial and in-service levels:

> In their initial training all teachers should have orientation to the constructive, indeed critical, role which they have in curriculum development. They should be encouraged to understand that their role is

not a passive one of merely transmitting the contents of syllabuses and textbooks into the heads of their pupils, but an active one involving decision making about the planning, implementation and evaluation of teaching activities . . . genuine involvement of teachers in curriculum development has to be stimulated through participatory forms of in-service training, with teachers planning their own activities and evaluating their own achievements. (1986: 225)

Avalos (1991: 31) argues that a participatory approach is ideally suited to in-service education because it is based on the analysis of previous experience of the trainees, their experience of teaching and their knowledge of the schools, the system and the local context. However, she notes that initial teacher training also offers possibilities for using reflection about prior school and context experience, and about experience they gain as their training proceeds through structured forms of field activities. Shaeffer (1990: 96–8) describes participatory teacher education as having the following general characteristics:

First, and above all, the teacher plays an active role in the training process and is therefore not a passive recipient of others' accumulated knowledge about methods and content. The teacher becomes a participant in decisions regarding the needs to which training must respond, what problems must be resolved and what skills and knowledge must be transmitted. The teacher becomes an agent rather than an object of change. Second, as a result of participation, training becomes self-directed and the teacher self-taught . . . Third, training is based on reflection and introspection. The teacher's needs, problems, status, role, etc. are not presented by outside observers or experts (supervisors and trainers) but are defined, examined and analysed by the teachers themselves . . . Fourth, participatory training bases introspection in the actual, concrete experiences of working with children in the classroom . . . Finally, . . . participatory training is often structured by the group. Teachers collectively examine and analyse their experiences, assisted by trainers . . . and so cooperate in solving problems and learning from each other.

Initial Teacher Education

Published evidence of more participant forms of initial teacher education is not very common, particularly in African countries. Even in Tanzania, where education for self-reliance should have created a context for such courses, the little evidence available is mixed. Kotta (1986) studied two colleges of education and found them to be over-reliant on lecturing and teacher-centred methods. However, research done by the writer at a teacher training college near to Dar Es Salaam (Harber, 1989: ch. 4) suggested that the students had experienced both active and passive learning methods, though there were differences within the college between different subject groups. However, when the students were asked the extent to which they thought that students rather than lecturers had been involved in deciding the content and methods of the course, the majority said that they had not been involved. The remainder of this section therefore examines case studies of participatory initial teacher education that have existed in Britain. Although in the light of democratisation the need for such courses and the participatory principles involved are universal, the need to adapt practices to particular local contexts and institutions must be borne in mind.

One such participatory course with which the writer was involved as one of two tutors was the Postgraduate Certificate of Education course at Birmingham University (Harber and Meighan, 1986; Meighan and Harber, 1986). Between 1976 and 1989 students were offered a choice between the familiar, authoritarian tutor-led course, an individualised, autonomous mode or a democratically run course. Nine of the twelve courses opted to organise themselves democratically. That is the group as a whole had the power to decide what would be learned, when and how and who would organise the learning. The groups opting for a democratic mode therefore tended to operate co-operatively in planning the course syllabus, allocating tasks and discussing and sharing ideas and materials for teaching methods. The preparation of course sessions frequently involved a division of labour with either individuals or small groups of two or three doing the work involved. Evaluations written by students during and at the end of the course suggested that such a learning method was perceived as having a number of major benefits. These can briefly be summarised as follows:

- learning by doing;
- congruence with the role of the teacher in the classroom;
- increased effort and responsibility;
- a very positive group atmosphere;
- increased confidence and increased motivation; and
- a wide range and variety of input.

Perhaps most importantly of all, feedback from both students and schools used for teaching practices provided convincing evidence that courses organised in such a manner help to create potentially better teachers. Teachers emerge who have both the skills necessary for survival and coping with the status quo (researching materials, formal instruction, discussion techniques and course planning and evaluation) but they also have a vision of possible alternative approaches based on their own experience. They have also gained some of the qualities of professionals: they have learned to work independently and as a team of co-operating equals, gained experience of decision making and the review of outcomes and they have developed personal confidence as well as the open-mindedness to assess the ideas and contributions of others in a constructive way.

Two other initial teacher education courses subsequently adapted this model to their own needs. The first was an early childhood PGCE course which was organised in this manner on two occasions. In evaluating the first course the group members were unanimous that it had been successful saying that they felt actively involved, motivated, had learned effectively and felt that their confidence and skills had been enhanced. The second group wrote down their observations under good features and bad features. Roughly 78 per cent of the comments were positive, 17 per cent negative and 5 per cent were devoted to speculative comment. The positive responses reiterated the themes already described above though, given the theme of education for democracy, it is important to note that they stressed the feeling of being free safely to express opinions since the role of the tutor was seen as non-judgemental. The negative points were the danger of some members dominating the group, the risk of unequal workloads and occasional sidetracking (Meighan, Harber and Meighan, 1989). Similar advantages and disadvantages were found by Abbot and Mercer (1989a, b) in their evaluation of a business studies teacher training course at the then Sunderland Polytechnic. All writers are clear, however, that both they and the students felt that the advantages greatly outweighed any disadvantages and indeed that some of the snags could have occurred with a traditional course while the benefits were unlikely to do so.

In-Service Teacher Education

Published accounts of participatory in-service education in developing countries are not so hard to come by and are well summarised by Shaeffer (1990). He divides these into four types of which two seem particularly relevant in the context of the attempt to use teacher education to alter school classrooms in a more democratic direction.

The first is the 'curriculum development' approach where teachers and trainees work together to establish needs, identify problems, suggest and evaluate possible solutions and, in so doing, develop new curricula, syllabuses, methods or texts. The teachers themselves are involved in curriculum development and change as practising teachers, and are trusted to do so because of the recognition that curriculum change is a daily occurrence in schools as teachers adapt to the problems that confront them. Such curriculum development models usually take place in either teachers' centres or teachers' workshops. Under the former category, for example, Shaeffer mentions Teacher Advisory Centres in Kenya and Botswana. Interestingly, he also mentions teacher workshops in South America (Chile, Argentina, Uraguay and Bolivia) which begun with the assumption that in order to transform the performance of teachers in the classroom, it is necessary to assist them to better understand the authoritarian and dogmatic role they currently play within the educational system and towards their students. Thus the teachers analyse extensively their own ability to work within the alternative, collective, non-authoritarian and non-dogmatic style of the workshop and then transfer this style to the classroom.

The second type is 'teacher as researcher' where teachers are encouraged to stand outside and critically examine their own taken for granted routines and practices (Shaeffer, 1990: 107–10). One example is from Kenya where secondary school teachers worked with a university lecturer to examine teaching problems, discuss teaching roles, analyse teacher motivation and performance and experiment with different teaching methods:

> Teacher participation in research in this study was envisaged at four levels. First, teachers were expected to get involved in planning and undertaking some of the logistical aspects of the research project such as collecting data from students in their classes, rating the quality of their own lessons, making themselves available for pre-active teaching interviews and other more general interviews. Second, the teachers were expected to participate in seminars where they would meet with teachers from other schools and undertake reflective discussions concerning two main issues: the factors within their school environment which might affect their work; and their own teaching practices as observed from video and audio recordings of their lessons. Third, the teachers were expected to identify areas within their practice which they felt needed to improve and, using both their own ideas as well as suggestions from their colleagues generated during the seminar discussions, implement observable instructional techniques designed to work towards improving selected teaching strategies. Lastly, the research participating teachers were expected to share their experiences about participation in the research with a larger audience of teachers to develop channels of dialogue among themselves in order to share experiences that might result in improving the quality of their practice.

Discussions in the project were frank and wide-ranging; points of view were clarified, attacked and defended; behaviours dissected and explained and alternative methods tried out.

Another example comes from Milton Margai Training College in Sierra Leone where a dozen lecturers were paired with an equal number of secondary school teachers to explore collaboratively a range of problems ranging from the teaching of local art to dropping out of the teaching profession. In one particular case, teachers were trained for a new integrated science programme in a traditional 'cookbook' or 'recipe' style. However, this was generally considered to be a failure. During later training, which was more collaborative in nature, teachers and researchers out-lined, elaborated and analysed a wide range of problems and worked out solutions to some of them. A further example occurred in Lesotho where five development studies teachers worked with a university researcher in describing and analysing classroom practice. Awareness of classroom processes was sharpened and the teachers gained insight into learning problems, added to their repertoire of skills and strategies, and increased their confidence and morale.

Shaeffer summarises the potential of this method for widening the horizons of teachers beyond acceptance of the 'normal' or 'traditional':

> Seeing their practice through outsiders' eyes, the teachers became aware of possibilities beyond the district curriculum and the established models of teaching and classroom structure. Changes occurred in how they redefined the task of teaching. Challenging what they once had perceived as constraints, they were able to seek answers and solutions to teaching dilemmas that were informed by their professional knowledge. (1990: 110)

A final example of a participatory in-service course is one recently run by the writer on the subject of teacher education for overseas students, mainly from developing countries, studying in Britain (Harber, 1993). This course ran for six years from 1989 to 1995 and none of the seventy-five or so students reported any experience of participatory methods in their initial teacher training, though a few had experienced them on short in-service courses. When, therefore, the case for a participant and co-operative course was put to them in the first meeting, that is that the students should decide what topics they would like covered, who would teach them and when, and that the tutor would act as a facilitator and adviser, it was perhaps not surprising that their reaction was often one of surprise and even alarm. Subsequent evaluations, however, highlighted similar advantages to those listed under initial teacher education (responsibility, interest, motivation, commitment, relevance and the importance of discussion) and, while some disadvantages were noted (time consuming, hard work for all, some sessions not as good as others) the students were clear that they preferred doing it this way and had valued the experience.

Conclusion

Both in Africa and internationally, authoritarian forms of teaching and learning in schools are much more common than democratic and participant ones. While there are a number of reasons for this, there is no doubt that teacher education tends to form part of an unvirtuous circle of authoritarian reproduction. Yet in the last six years democracy has asserted itself on the world stage as the general form of government to which all countries should now aspire, even if there are still major hurdles in the way of its final achievement. If these hurdles are to be overcome in Africa and democracy made sustainable, then states will need to promote education more consciously aimed at the development of democratic values and the protection of human rights via greater discussion and participation. This will require not only re-schooling for democratic political development but also the re-education of teachers and consequently the teacher educators themselves. As the discussion in this chapter has demonstrated, we are not without examples of how teacher education can be made more democratic, co-operative and participant. How to move away from over-reliance on uncritical knowledge transmission and technical skills training to forms of democratic teacher education should now be a central question for teacher educators in Africa and elsewhere.

8

'The Struggle Itself was a School': Education and Independence in Eritrea

Eritrea became independent in 1991 after one hundred years of colonialism and after a brutal thirty-year liberation war against its neighbour Ethiopia in which 150,000 of its people died and another 100,000 were either disabled or orphaned (Paice, 1994: 26). This has been viewed as the first-break up of an African state since the Charter of the Organisation of African Unity stated its determination to 'safeguard and consolidate . . . the sovereignty and territorial integrity of our states'. In fact, the Charter was greatly influenced by the then Ethiopian Emperor Haile Selassie, who had recently annexed Eritrea after a period of 'federation', the OAU argument that colonial boundaries be respected actually supported Eritrea's claim to independence as its borders were established during Italian colonisation.

The phrase 'the struggle itself was a school' comes from Haile Woldetensai, a leading member of the Eritrean People's Liberation Front (Connel, 1993: 244) and it is certainly the case that education played a significant role in Eritrea's struggle for independence and must play an equally important part in supporting the democratic structures that are now being discussed and created. However, post-independence educational debates, including those on education for democracy, will inevitably be influenced by both the positive and negative educational experiences of the colonial period. In order to understand these experiences it is at first necessary to provide a brief outline of modern Eritrean history. Apart from relevant documentary sources this chapter is also informed by many discussions with Eritrean education students between 1992 and 1994, the written work of some of these students on democracy and political education and a research visit to Eritrea in January 1995.

Eritrea, 1890–1991

After a period of gradual incursion during the 1880s Italy formally established a colony in Eritrea in 1890 and it remained so until the Italians were defeated by the British during the Second World War in 1941. This fifty-year period shaped and defined the Eritrean identity:

> People from diverse economic, ethnic and religious backgrounds were structurally linked within the colonial borders. Their experiences differed sharply from those of their neighbours in Ethiopia. Ethiopia remained dominated by a feudal economic system managed by imperial rule. By the 1940s Eritrea had developed a substantial working class as well as a distinct urban-based intelligentsia. Access to information about world events was enhanced by the presence of Italy and Italian settlers and by the expansion of trade and international exchange. (Government of Eritrea, 1993: 9)

Although the British Military Administration which ruled Eritrea between 1941 and 1950 was set on policy of partition with western and northern Eritrea going to Sudan and the rest to Ethiopia, this was rejected by the newly-formed United Nations and the debate moved on to whether to join all of Eritrea to Ethiopia or to give it independence as had happened in Italy's other African colonies, Libya and Somaliland. However, Eritrea's fate was sealed by the increasingly close relationship developing between America and Ethiopia. America's interest in Eritrea was primarily concerned with cold war strategy as the US representative John Foster Dulles made clear during a Security Council debate in 1950:

> From the point of view of justice, the opinions of the Eritrean people must receive consideration. Nevertheless, the strategic interests of the US in the Red Sea basin and considerations of security and world peace make it necessary that this country has to be linked to our ally, Ethiopia. (Government of Eritrea, 1993: 14)

Despite electoral evidence that the Eritrean people did not favour such a federation (Paice, 1994: 28), the UN passed a US-backed plan for federation which went into effect from 15 September 1952. In 1953, the US and Ethiopia signed two agreements that gave America a twenty-five year lease on military and intelligence bases in Eritrea and pledged America to provide military aid and training to Ethiopia. Much of this military assistance and training was later used to fight the Eritrean liberation movement.

During the 1950s there followed a period of the gradual annexation of Eritrea by Ethiopia. Newspapers were closed, political activists, journalists and trade unionists arrested and local languages banned. Police were present in the National Assembly which was surrounded by Ethiopian military forces during critical votes. In 1962 the Ethiopian emperor Haile Selassie declared that the federal period was terminated. The impossibility of peaceful political activity meant that there was little alternative to armed struggle and this led to the formation of the Eritrean Liberation Front. During the 1970s, however, and particularly after a brief civil war in the early 1980s, the Eritrean People's Liberation Front emerged as the dominant liberation movement. Unlike the ELF the EPLF was committed not only to independence but also to a process of radical social change not simply after independence but during the war itself, and its policies were put into effect in the liberated zones it controlled.

In 1974 Haile Selassie was ousted in a military coup which resulted in a military government in Ethiopia known by its Amharic name as the 'Dergue' and led by Mengistu Haile Meriam. This Marxist-Leninist inspired regime launched a policy of state terrorism against the Ethiopian people, particularly between 1976 and 1978, which became known as the 'Red Terror'. It also intensified the war against the Eritrean liberation movement. However, by 1977 Ethiopia was on the brink of defeat in Eritrea with the freedom fighters controlling most of the countryside and many major towns. At this point the Ethiopians turned to the then Soviet Union which saw the Marxist regime in Addis Ababa as a potential ally in cold-war terms and over the next seventeen years the Soviet Union provided Ethiopia with the equivalent of 12 billion US dollars in military equipment and training (Government of Eritrea, 1993: 18), much of which now lies rusting in huge 'tank graveyards' around Eritrean towns and cities. Soviet intervention turned the tide of the war and the EPLF was forced to retreat to its base in the north-east Sahel region.

However, Mengistu's forced conscription policy left him with an army of poorly trained, badly informed and poorly motivated soldiers who had little idea of why they were fighting the war. Thus, despite massive superiority in terms of manpower and technology and with the EPLF having to rely solely on weapons captured from the Ethiopians or made by themselves, the Ethiopian offensives of the 1980s gradually faltered against the highly motivated and disciplined EPLF fighters. With the increasing success of the EPLF and the collapse of its ally the Soviet Union the Ethiopian army was in serious trouble until on 24 May 1991 the capital Asmara finally fell to the EPLF.

Education Under Italian and British Rule

Negash (1987: ch. 3) has identified three periods of Italian colonial education policy. During the first period (1897–1907) the Italian governor of Eritrea, Ferdinando Martini, saw any education as a threat to colonialism as colonies could only be kept by a strict separation of the races, by the cultivation of European prestige in relation to the colonised and by denying the indigenous population access to western education. This policy of no schooling for Eritreans was changed by Martini's successor, Salvago-Raggi, who opened state primary schools in order to produce sufficiently educated workers for the postal and telegraphic services and no more. In 1916 the Italian government in Rome issued a policy document on colonial education which among other things made it clear that native education was to be limited to the equivalent of the first three years of elementary education in Italy. Education would therefore serve the needs of the colonial state but would not be provided to the point where critical ideas might become a risk to Italian control of the colony.

During the third period from 1934, with Italy now controlled by fascists, education was seen as useful for consolidating and supporting colonial rule. The Superintendent of Schools in 1934 said that:

> The child ought to know something of our civilisation in order to make him a conscious propagandist among the families who live far away inland. And through our educational policy, the native should know of Italy, her glories and her ancient history in order to become a conscious militant behind the shadow of our flag. (Negash, 1987: 71)

In keeping with fascist ideology which had led to the imposition of strict racial segregation in the colony in 1937, racist arguments were added to tactical ones as to why education should be limited for native Eritreans. Africans were seen as pathologically inferior to Europeans and therefore unable to rule Africa to Europe's satisfaction. Textbooks in use during the period of Italian colonisation stressed the greatness of Italy, the civilising benefits of colonial government, improvements in the economy since colonisation and the non-existence of pre-colonial history in the Eritrean region. While, therefore, the school in Eritrea as an Italian colony was always an elite institution in the sense that it was accessible at most to 2 per cent of the population, it nevertheless prevented the emergence of an Eritrean intellectual elite by limiting education to the elementary level and providing indoctrination rather than education.

While the period of British rule from 1941 to 1950 can be seen in some ways as a welcome respite from Italian fascist rule, particularly in terms of the repeal of racial laws, it was also the period that witnessed the first stirrings of Eritrean nationalism. The defeat of the colonial power, a downturn in the post-war economy, continuing resentment over land that had been appropriated, the return of politically conscious Eritrean soldiers form the war in Libya and elsewhere and the general post-war interest in independence in Africa provided a context in which Eritrean nationalism could thrive:

> And it is in this period, towards the end of outright colonial rule and in the period of British provisional government, that the constellation of nationalities which had long formed the Eritrean population began – as elsewhere in Africa – to come to terms with the concept of a common nationhood, and therefore a common nationalism. (Davidson, 1980: 13)

Moreover, modest increases in educational opportunity in the form of the opening of sixty new schools and a teacher-training institution (Trevaskis, 1960: 35; Paice, 1994: 25) led to dissatisfaction expressing itself more and more in political awareness and activity. As it became clear that Britain would not honour its promises of freedom made in leaflets dropped by the Royal Air Force at the outbreak of hostilities, political agitation began to take more organised forms. This was made possible because the British allowed a measure of freedom of speech and association, and established an active press and information service which published and broadcast in English, Tigrinya and Arabic. This led to the emergence of political commentators such as Wolde-Ab Wolde-Mariam whose writing on the future of Eritrea was widely read and debated, especially in the urban centres. However:

> Mass consciousness and participation was not limited to the urban centres. Village schools were mushrooming, in addition to those in the cities, under a crash programme organised and directed by an energetic British education officer. This produced in rapid succession crops of literate youngsters who helped in the spread of political education through daily reading of newspaper articles to parents. In this way, ideas and opinions were communicated effectively, and names like Wolde-Ab became household words together with what they stood for. (Selassie, 1980: 36)

Education Under Ethiopia

While the number of schools in Eritrea grew rapidly in the 1950s, student unrest also grew in the light of continued Ethiopian violation of human rights. In 1956 students intermittently boycotted classes and in 1957 took to the streets when Tigrinya and Arabic were replaced by Amharic, the official Ethiopian language. When students failed in Amharic they lost the opportunity of pursuing further and higher education – even if they had good results in other subjects. Eritrean students failed because the language was alien to them and they were less motivated to learn it because of their antipathy towards it.

After annexation in 1962 matters became even worse:

> Onwards from 1962 the Ethiopian regime governed, or attempted to govern, Eritrea on straightforward colonial lines: that is, with the introduction of Amharic authority at all decisive points; with the suppression in education and public life of Tigrinya and other local languages in favour of the Amharic language; with the exclusion of any specific Eritrean identity, right to decision, or control over local development; and, increasingly, with the use of military force to suppress all signs or claims of Eritrean independence. (Davidson, 1980: 14)

In education the main aim of the new curriculum introduced in 1963 was to Ethiopianise Eritreans and Ethiopian school textbooks, and teachers were imported in order to achieve this. Two Eritreans, now senior educationalists, recall their experience of schools at this time:

> When I was a student in the Ethiopian government school in history lessons we were taught that Ethiopia was a country that had enjoyed '3,000 years of freedom' and that Eritrea was 'part and parcel of Ethiopia from time immemorial'. The emperor was portrayed as 'a heroic leader who liberated both Eritreans and Ethiopians from Italy's fascism'. We studied Ethiopia's sovereignty and its kings, queens etc. Hence, they always wanted to make a scapegoat of European colonialism while replacing them in the same manner or even worse. In geography lessons Eritrea was mentioned as the 14th province of Ethiopia; that it was occupied by the Italians 'temporarily' and that in 1963 Eritrea 'voluntarily' united with its 'motherland' and 'not annexed' as was the case. We used to memorise what was written in our note-books without question and produced these again during exams. (Teklu, 1993: 11–12)

> I remember studying Ethiopian history and geography as if Eritrea didn't have its own. In Ethiopian history we were taught that Ethiopia is the owner of 3,000 years of continuous independence and Eritrea is mentioned as an integral part of Ethiopia since antiquity. Portraits of the emperor and other members of the royal family were displayed everywhere, in classrooms, textbooks and even exercise books. We were forced to sing the Ethiopian national anthem and other songs which praised His Imperial Majesty Haile Selassie 1. The schools were authoritarian and hierarchical and thus teacher–student relationships were not healthy. Since corporal punishment was permissible, most teachers beat their students brutally. Classroom methods were always one way, i.e. the 'talk and chalk' method. Students were expected to memorise word by word the short notes they copied from the blackboard. Those who did not repeat the words fluently were beaten

cruelly and were made to go into other classes with posters like 'I am a donkey' or 'I am ignorant' hanging form their backs. (Almedom, 1994: 10–11)

After the overthrow of Haile Selassie in 1974 by the Marxist-Leninist inspired military, the government began to tighten its grip on education as a potential focus of resistance. During the period of the red terror between 1977 and 1978 not only were 30,000 Ethiopians executed for political reasons but in a period of just one month police and army squads murdered five thousand school children and university students. School children and university students caught demonstrating were gunned down on the spot (Tesfagiorgis, 1992: 137). Eritrea did not escape such events. In January 1975, for example, 100 young people were strangled with wire by the Dergue authorities in Asmara (Government of Eritrea, 1993: 17).

Eritrean teachers were transferred to other parts of Ethiopia and replaced by Ethiopians. Spies and informers within both the staff and student body created mistrust and tension – those suspected of working for liberation were regularly arrested and tortured. The control of schools by individual headteachers was minimised by strengthening ministerial control over what happened in schools. When the military regime created the Ethiopian Workers' Party (EWP), which was the sole party in Ethiopia, headteachers were also forced to become party members. Some teachers also became members which further heightened tensions beween those loyal to the regime and those suspected of being sympathetic to the liberation movement. The EWP established offices in every school and issued guidelines about the ways in which schools should be organised. The military regime also encouraged mass promotion regardless of competence so that students, especially those who failed and were frustrated, would not join the liberation front. Many schools in both rural and urban areas were confiscated by the Ethiopian army and used as barracks; consequently, these schools bear the scars of battle today (Teklu, 1993; Tesfamariam 1993).

Schooling became geared to the orthodoxies of Ethiopian Marxism. A consultancy report on primary education published soon after independence, for example, contains a picture of a school wall at Himberti with a large placard of Marx, Engels and Lenin (Woldemichael,1992). Curricular content also became aimed at creating socialist cadres. Even a brief glance at history questions used for the Ethiopian school-leaving examination in history, for example, demonstrates this quite clearly through the language employed and the consistent use of class analysis.

However, the use of marxist analysis in multiple choice questions adds a bizarre, almost comical, element to the attempt at indoctrination in the contrast between highly complex historical questions and a series of possible one-line 'factual' answers:

> The 1848–9 revolutions showed:
> A. that in Europe the bourgeoisie was no longer a revolutionary force
> B. that national quarrels were fatal to the success of revolutionary movements
> C. that an alliance of the workers and peasants was necessary for the success of revolutionary movements
> D. all of the above
> E. B and C above.
>
> The economic crisis of 1857 in Europe and the USA was a new kind of crisis, typical of capitalism, a crisis caused by:
> A. shortage of labour power
> B. inflation
> C. shortage of raw materials
> D. harvest failure
> E. over production
>
> The social basis of opportunism within the international socialist movement before World War 1 was:
> A. the lumpen proletariat
> B. the intelligentsia
> C. national minorities
> D. rural wage workers
> E. the worker's (labour) aristocracy. (Admasu and Alemayehu, 1994)

Political education was also introduced as a school subject in order to socialise students into Marxist-Leninism. Interestingly, Tesfamariam (1993) notes that when the concepts of democracy and equality were taught they were deliberately misinterpreted and inculcated in a negative way to mean the absence of any rules at all. Truancy, for example, which was understandably high at the time, was described as a form of democracy as part of giving it a negative connotation. Not surprisingly, education in Eritrea in the Mengistu period became demoralised and the fear and resentment of many young people led to them running away to join the liberation movement. As one Eritrean mother whose own two daughters also eventually joined the 'tegadelti' (fighters) put it:

> It was at this time that young boys and girls, most of them of high school age, joined the fronts in such large numbers that many had to be turned away. Mothers actively encouraged their children to go. It was better to fight for a worthy cause, the parents reasoned, and face death with their brothers and sisters in the struggle, than stay at home and hope to evade the wolves. (Tesfagiorgis, 1992: 20)

Political Education and the EPLF

This section will focus on the education policies and practices of the Eritrean People's Liberation Front. It will do so for two reasons. First, it was the EPLF that eventually emerged as the dominant liberation organisation and won the war of liberation. Thus its educational policies will be important in independent Eritrea. Secondly, unlike the Eritrean Liberation Front, the EPLF believed in social revolution and transformation during the war rather than waiting until military victory was secured. Education therefore played a very important part in the liberation struggle. While many aspects of education were treated very seriously by the EPLF, in particular basic literacy in the mother tongue and the learning of common languages such as Tigrinya, Arabic and English, the overall educational effort was also political and geared towards the new kind of Eritrea that the EPLF wanted to create. As the American Dan Connel, one of the few Western journalists reporting from Eritrea during the war, put it in his book *Against All Odds*:

> What pulled me back again and again was the unique social experiment that Eritrea is – both for itself and for the world. The liberation movement's main achievement was the direct engagement of much of the Eritrean civilian population in the process of social change and nation-building. The main themes of this book centre on that process – on Eritrean efforts to create a functioning democracy, unique in Africa, with broad social equality and popular participation across clan, ethnic, religious, gender and class lines. (1993: 50)

In January 1977 the EPLF held its first Organisational Congress which adopted a National Democratic Programme. Its eleven objectives were: to establish a people's democratic state; to build an independent, self-reliant and planned national economy; to develop culture, education, technology and public health; to safeguard social rights; to ensure the equality and consolidate the unity of nationalities; to build a strong people's army; to respect freedom of religion and faith; provide humane treatment for prisoners of war and encourage the desertion of Eritrean soldiers serving the enemy; to protect the rights of Eritreans living abroad; to respect the rights of foreigners residing in Eritrea; and to pursue a common policy of peace and non-alignment (Wilson, 1991: 99). It was clear that in order to begin to construct such a new society, a massive change in outlook and beliefs would be required. Eritreans would need to come to see social realities not as immutable and inevitable but as shaped and created by human beings. This would require widespread programmes of political education both among citizens of all ages in the towns and villages of the liberated zones and among school students in the EPLF's own schools. The remainder of this section will examine political education in general while the next section will focus on the EPLF's Zero or Revolution School.

Political education carried out by the EPLF among the general population took two forms: education by practice and example, and more formal political presentations. In the case of the former the EPLF went about politicising the population through its role in the social and economic life of the liberated zones. The EPLF ran plantations, new co-operative stores, small workshops, field clinics, schools and elaborate underground supply depots. EPLF doctors and mobile agricultural extension workers through their work would open a dialogue with individual peasants on political issues. Military units stopped in the fields to help peasants and to talk politics informally with them. EPLF shops and stores increased the front's profile by providing basic services and by engaging people in the running of the institutions, which served as examples of co-operative politics. Connell observed how the EPLF operated in one village:

> During the time I spent in Zagher in 1976–8, much of the contact I observed between these cadres and the villagers was informal – in the fields, by the stream, over coffee in the afternoons or simply squatting in the dirt somewhere in the village. The organizers were humble and unhurried. They listened well. They joked and teased. They also gave concrete advice on how to increase crop yields, and they gave villagers new seed varieties and new crops such as flowers that could be sold in the towns. They bought a motor and other equipment for the grain mill, and they provided several white leghorns to the women for their poultry project. Most importantly, they never took a thing from the villagers without asking first and then paying for it. People in Zagher trusted these earnest organisers; more than this they liked them. Often members of the EPLF team visited villagers in their home to chat with no agenda other than to promote dialogue and to listen. (1993: 120)

As a result, when Zagher was occupied by the Dergue's troops in the late 1970s and offered fertilizers, pipes and mills resistance was firm. As one man said at the first meeting with the Ethiopians:

> The fighters built us mills. They were teaching us politics. They gave us free medication. Five kilos of grain used to cost five birr in Asmara. They made a co-operative shop and sold it for two-fifty. They brought us kerosene, oil, onions and coffee with their trucks. In these four years, we didn't know imprisonment or insults – everything was solved by understanding and criticism–self-criticism and we governed ourselves by a people's assembly. (Connell, 1993: 185)

Political education was also taught in a more formal way to both civilians and fighters and was a constant feature of life in EPLF areas.

In the city of Keren, for example, in one weekly period more than fifty political education meetings were held in the six zones of the city. Not only the general populace underwent such training but also most of the lower and middle-level government officials were 'rehabilitated' through the process of political education (Sherman, 1980: 105). While such political education stressed Eritrean history and the importance of national unity in the midst of ethnic diversity, its economic and political message in the 1970s and early 1980s was clearly Marxist socialist. This was due to a number of factors. At that time Marxist socialism was the obvious, indeed only, ideology for those interested in revolution and particularly for the young student militants who joined the EPLF and had been through higher education in the late 1960s when student politics were heavily influenced by the works of Marx, Lenin, Mao, Trotsky and Guevara. Moreover, those Middle Eastern and African regimes that supported the liberation movement – Sudan, Somalia, Algeria, Libya, Iraq, the Palestine Liberation Organisation and the People's Democratic Republic of Yemen all had left-leaning governments.

The political education course provided at this time was not only socialist but also rather doctrinaire, authoritarian and one way in the way it was taught. Connell (1993: 104–5) describes one political education meeting in Decamare:

> A bearded, khaki-clad EPLF cadre was illustrating how workers were exploited in their jobs when I walked into the crowded schoolroom to observe. Some thirty-five industrial workers sat attentively at desks that were far too small for them, staring at the blackboard . . . The young organiser argued that the basic interests of workers and owners were diametrically opposed – only social revolution would bring about lasting change. 'If the struggle is going to succeed, the workers must first get organised, conscious and united. You must know who are your friends and who are your enemies, and you must build a national alliance against colonial oppression as well. In this mass association you will learn to do this.'

However, by the mid-1980s changes had begun to take place in EPLF ideology and political education. The nature of the Mengistu regime in Addis Ababa undermined faith in Marxist certainties and the famine of this period meant increasing exposure to Western ideas through the activities of the many charities and non-governmental organisations that came to the region. Moreover, by the second half of the 1980s the clear signs of ideological retreat in the Soviet Union undermined this model of political and economic development. The change in the EPLF was reflected in the second organisational congress held in March 1987. At this conference not only was some of the old, more extreme language abandoned but the movement was formally committed to multi-party politics after independence; discussions on the floor of the congress were open, with participants encouraged to raise issues, ask questions, challenge the leadership and debate among themselves. Connell describes how by 1990 this change in the EPLF affected the emphasis in political education which shifted from the 1970s language and orthodoxies of Marxism/socialism to multi-party democracy, a mixed economy, social justice and national unity. Moreover, the style of political education was less strident, less based on polemic, formulas and slogans and more open and two way, reflecting a change from 'vanguard' revolutionary politics of the war to the imminence of an independent and democratic state (1993: 299–40, 243–4, 273–5).

A key issue of social justice in political education throughout the struggle was the question of gender equality. This reflected the role that women played in the armed conflict: by the end of the war one-third of all fighters were women. One woman fighter made the following connection between gender equality, democratic freedoms and human rights:

> So now we have a woman company commander: she does not command only women but men and women. At least 200 men are under her. There are many women company commanders, squad commanders and platoon commanders. This is not done just for the sake of rights for women but because Eritreans are fighting for freedom and to fight for freedom you have to have your rights. When the first women joined in 1973 the men thought 'What can they do, these women?' Then the men saw what women could do – in the clinics and as dressers and at the front line. They saw them fight, take prisoners, capture tanks; they saw them when they lost their legs, their eyes. Then they stopped talking about women, now they accept women. (Wilson, 1991: 98–9)

EPLF policy on women's rights amounted to the social transformation of a traditionally patriarchal society. The EPLF programme included, for example, a commitment to free women from domestic confinement, full rights of equality in politics, economy and social life, equal pay for equal work, progressive marriage and family laws, the right to two months' maternity leave with full pay, the eradication of prostitution, and programmes to increase and upgrade the quality of women leaders and public servants (Davidson, Cliffe and Selassie, 1980: 147). In the liberated areas the EPLF were successful in halting the practice of female 'circumcision' (genital mutilation) through an education campaign and in 1977 adopted a marriage law that applied directly to members but which was also intended as a model for civil society. This banned child betrothal and child marriage and abolished the dowry and bride price. Such issues and policies became an important part of structured political education and discussion (Connell, 1993: 132, 135).

The Zero School

The EPLF ran a number of schools in the liberated areas but the Zero School (also known as the Revolution School) was the main EPLF educational centre and was also used for teacher education and curriculum development. As with SWAPO's Loudima School, it is therefore important in understanding the likely direction of education policy in independent Eritrea. It was opened in 1976 and the classrooms and dormitories were built into a mountain or camouflaged under trees to protect them from air raids. The school started with 250 children but by the early 1980s it had grown to 2,500 and by the late 1980s to 4,000 (Dines, 1980: 136; Kinnock, 1988: 35).

Political education was part of the curriculum from the start. However, as the EPLF lacked experience and trained teachers early attempts at the political education of young people presented many problems. The syllabus was full of difficult concepts and theories and the texts full of jargon. Topics such as revolution, criticism and self-criticism, democracy and imperialism were taught from grade one. Moreover, teaching method was still rigid and based on lectures. As one EPLF teacher put it 'how difficult it is for a child of seven to follow a 40-minute lecture on revolutionary discipline can be imagined!' (Almedon 1994). However, in 1982 a new political education syllabus was introduced as part of an Eritrean national curriculum. This aimed to simplify the content and started at grade 3 rather than grade 1. The content of political education included both the armed struggle and the peaceful political struggle, the cultures of all ethnic groups, the concepts of the state, colonialism, democracy, classes and society and the situation in Eritrea, the Horn of Africa, the Middle East and the Cold War. Important aims included helping the students to gain in self-confidence, to make them understand that everybody should be equal and should be given equal opportunities, to show that the real enemies of Eritrea were the Ethiopian government and not the Ethiopian people, and to help them not to become suspicious of foreigners so that they don't end up by being racist themselves (EPLF, 1982: 19–20).

Moreover, both in political education and in other subjects teaching methods began to change from the early 1980s onwards. As the director of the Zero School from 1982–91 put it:

When we started to teach the students . . . we practiced the traditional way of teaching, i.e. chalk and talk. Here we did not give the students the chance to participate. Almost the whole period was dominated by the teacher without stopping in-between to give them time to ask. The method was a sort of spoon feeding and hence we did not allow the students to investigate, examine, to conclude for themselves and to acquire skills . . . [whereas later] . . . Attempts were made to apply a more child-centred approach and to promote problem solving methods and become more participatory. This was more or less adopted from the democratic approach of Paulo Freire. Therefore, training was conducted and discussions and seminars were carried out. Here we have to note that whenever new ideas or innovations came all the teachers discussed it and finally if they agreed and were convinced they implemented it. This was especially true regarding the fighters who were highly motivated and who had a great desire to put democracy into effect. (Tesfamariam, 1993: 9–10)

Tesfamariam also notes how assessment was changed to weaken the pressures of examinations. During the colonial period examinations were aimed at eliminating the majority of students in order to produce an elite. It was also used by teachers as a weapon to punish students they did not like. In the Zero and other EPLF schools in the liberated zones continuous assessment was integrated into the whole teaching/learning process so that it comprised 60 per cent of the marks whereas 40 per cent were allocated to examinations. In marking a regulation was introduced that teachers should stop writing 'bad', 'poor' and 'excellent' in exercise books. Instead a mark and encouraging comments, advice and guidelines were given. Monthly meetings were held by teachers to evaluate every student's achievement as well as psychological and social problems.

If students had problems extra remedial classes were organised and individual follow up, counselling and consultation were carried out. This was done continuously until the students could cope in normal classes.

Moreover, in the Zero School students were fully involved in decision making through a series of school committees such as the production committee, the seminar committee, the disciplinary committee, the sports committee, and the recreation committee. Students in the school were organised according to their ages, e.g. 7–12, 13–15 and 16. Each age group was also divided into teams which consisted of 50–60 students. It was from these teams that students were elected to the committees. For example, the production committee was elected by those who were sixteen years old and above so each one of the five teams from this age group chose one representative. There was also a teacher on the committee. Production was organised once a week by the committee and the students and teachers worked together.

Each week the committee held a meeting to discuss the work that needed to be done – constructing houses, repairing roads, digging wells and fetching firewood – and who would do it. Hence, they were responsible for organising the work and prioritising the tasks and they had the power to either implement or reject demands coming from the staff or the headteacher. Another example of a committee was the seminar committee. The main task of this committee was to prepare topics for fortnightly seminars. Issues discussed openly and freely at these seminars included discipline, relationships inside the school, the future and school administration as well as political issues like unity, democracy and equality.

Also, apart from the overall committees, every month team and classroom meetings were held. At the elementary level the class teacher was present to chair the meeting. At these meetings the teaching-learning process, student to student relationships and staff–student relationships were discussed. The class teacher was responsible for reporting the outcome to a meeting of the whole staff where students' criticisms and suggestions were discussed and taken seriously by the staff. At the junior and senior secondary level class meetings were conducted according to grades or year in school. During such meetings teaching and learning were discussed critically and suggestions made. When the teachers wanted to talk they raised their hands and were controlled by the chairperson in the same manner as everyone else. As the director of the school concluded:

> Therefore, the Zero School tried to make decisions collectively and encouraged the students to participate actively and trained them to be good citizens who were free to give suggestions and opinions . . . students were responsible and disciplined and their academic achievement was high but beyond this they were tolerant and critical. Even now they are participating actively in Eritrean politics and are the ardent supporters of democracy. (Tesfamariam, 1993: 14)

Others have commented favourably on the nature of the school. Firebrace and Holland (1985: 120) described the students as 'enthusiastic and well-motivated'. Sherman (1980: 105) reported the way 'Eritrea's nine nationalities show great enthusiasm to learn from and integrate with one another. Free from narrow nationalist or chauvinist thinking, they are forging deep unity among the nationalities'. When the British Labour politician Glenys Kinnock visited the school in 1988 she was impressed by what she found in terms of the commitment to equal opportunities, the emphasis on a co-operative, non-competitive approach, the absence of externally imposed discipline and that the students and teachers were encouraged to value and respect each other. Her concluding observation was:

> And if it sounds idyllic, it certainly wasn't. The place, the conditions, the war forbid that. But as an experienced teacher, I have to say that even in the many good schools that I know, I've never seen teacher–pupil relationships like those I saw among the sticks and stones of Zero School. (Kinnock, 1988: 40)

After the war some 500 students from the Zero School, many of whom had lost one or both parents in the war, were moved to a new site at Decamare some forty kilometres from Asmara. Here they attend a local school but live in dormitories in what was until 1991 an Ethiopian army base. The writer visited the school in January 1995 in the company of its director from 1982 to 1991 and found that the domestic arrangements have retained much of the ethos of the Zero School. The dormitories are ethnically mixed, there is a strongly co-operative and friendly atmosphere. There is a council composed of elected representatives from the dormitories which meets once a month but can meet weekly if issues arise. However, the students, like those from the Loudima School in Namibia, expressed their concerns about the problems of integrating into the local 'normal' school. These students are used to very committed teachers who treat them as equals and discuss matters in a participatory manner. They pointed out that whereas teachers in the Zero School would encourage questions, even if they were not particularly good ones, the teachers in the present school discouraged questions and even scolded them if they asked. Also, the strong bonds of trust and camaraderie were not present in the local school, where there were incidents of stealing and fighting.

Education and the Politics of Independence

The post-independence Provisional Government of Eritrea is committed to the principle of democracy, as this statement from the government makes clear:

> The EPLF and the PGE have acted on their commitment to democratisation. This pledge is not born of a desire to respond to current international trends. It is part of a history of democratic struggle that began in the 1940s and continued through the period of armed struggle . . . Elections, for example, are not new to the many Eritreans who lived in EPLF administered areas during the war. There, the principles of religious freedom, women's equality and human rights were actively practiced . . . While democracy has strong roots in Eritrea, its thorough application cannot be determined by a formula or time-tables. Given the unmatched importance of democratic structures and

policies in Eritrea's future, flexibility and thoroughness are critical. Emphasis must be given to building and expanding democracy from the bottom up. It cannot be imposed from the top by creating formal national structures without a base in society. (Government of Eritrea, 1993: 30)

Accordingly, the referendum of the future status of Eritrea was held democratically in 1993 and Presidential and parliamentary elections are promised for 1997. Also, as an observer at the first international symposium on the making of the Eritrean constitution in January 1995, the writer can attest to the firm determination to create democratic government in Eritrea. However, there are three important issues that arise in relation to this statement about democracy. The first is that although democracy was indeed a major aim of the independence struggle the nature of such democracy was not clear during the period when Marx and Lenin were at the height of their influence in the EPLF. As in Tanzania, democracy could have sat uncomfortably with a one-party state. The change to acceptance of multi-party democracy has come about, at least in part, as a result of changing world and African circumstances. The second is the emphasis on human rights and religious freedom. The toleration necessary for this is already being sorely tested in Eritrea. During the struggle Jehovah's Witnesses refused to take part in the fighting, did not take part in the referendum and have shunned national service. As a result in the face of understandable widespread bitterness against them the government stripped them of citizenship in December 1994 so that they can no longer hold government jobs or Eritrean passports (*The Guardian*, 23 May 1995).

Controversies about conscientious objectors have been a feature of the histories of many countries are not easily or simply resolved. Nevertheless, Jehovah's Witnesses do not pose a threat to the state and the removal of citizenship does not deny the right to religious freedom. The strength of a government and people in a democratic state can be judged by what they can tolerate rather than what they can close down. Abeba Tesfagiorgis, an Eritrean woman who is a former political prisoner of the Dergue, makes an interesting point in this regard in her autobiography. In prison she tells the true story of a French woman Irene Laure' who was active in the resistance in the Second World War and saw many of her friends tortured but who learned to forgive the Germans. She comments to fellow prisoners that:

just as Irene Laure' could not hope to see a united and peaceful Europe without Germany, we could not say we loved our country and then refuse to understand and forgive our fellow Eritreans. (Tesfagiorgis, 1992: 56)

Both of these two issues are relevant to the third – the need to develop a democratic civil society as well as democratic constitutional political structures. This is the argument that democratic rules and institutions will only thrive and survive if embedded in a population of politically informed citizens who understand the political choices in front of them, and where there exists a political culture based on democratic values that tolerates, and even celebrates, diversity. As has been argued throughout this book, democratic knowledge, skills and values have to be learned and education must therefore play a key part. As one Eritrean writer has recently put it:

> In order for democracy to succeed Eritreans must be socialised not merely mobilised to democratic values . . . Democracy – a messy business at best – requires that individual rights, liberties, diverse opinions, and interests be taken into consideration simultaneously with the collective good. If the Eritrean government does not succumb to the temptation to overvalue order and stability, and thus curb the sphere of political participation, the population can be socialised to live with the happy uncertainties of democracy. (Iyob, 1995: 146)

Two key policy documents on moral and civic education since independence (Institute of Curriculum Development, 1992, 1993) make a commitment to political education for democracy clear. The first document outlines the EPLF's experience of school-based political education from 1977 to 1988 and concludes that it was too difficult for students of the ages concerned. It suggests that the newly termed civic education should aim at the creation of participant and responsible citizens who value equality, freedom and democratic justice:

> This will secure a continuity of correct outlook towards the common good and prevent violations of the rights of the individual by the government or any other bodies. It will foster the development of understanding, which would enable them to examine and decide common issues and use their knowledge properly. (Institute of Curriculum Development, 1992: 8)

However, while it lists content for civic education (basically local, national and international political institutions) and the need to develop critical thinking, there is little on the teaching methods needed to develop democratic political skills or explore political values.

The second document makes clear the influence of the experience of the Zero or revolution School, including the need to introduce democratic and progressive practices. It is clearly directed towards educating about democratic political institutions, including a multiparty system as long as the parties are not based on ethnicity or regionalism; it is also clear that desirable traits such as honesty, responsibility, the work ethic, and self-reliance cannot and should not be indoctrinated but rather require open education, reason and good example. There is more than in the first document on the desirability of participation through variety in teaching method but nothing on the important issue of assessment.

Conclusion

After a long and bitter war Eritrea has clearly decided on a path of democracy and human rights. Despite the use of Marxist-Leninist rhetoric during the struggle against Ethiopia, the EPLF was, like SWAPO, always primarily a nationalist movement and it has been flexible over the years in adapting its thinking according to Eritrea's needs in the light of changing times and circumstances. This has also been the pattern with education. From early sloganeering and didactic and authoritarian teaching methods education in the Zero School gradually changed to become more critical, two-way and participatory – in a word more democratic. Moreover, the Zero School also provided a useful democratic model for school management in independent Eritrea. Many senior educationalists in Eritrea were fighters and EPLF teachers. They know each other well and there is a cohesive ideology in favour of democratisation and social justice in terms of equality of opportunity for both genders and for all ethnic groups. The first educational policy documents that have emerged such as those on civics and moral education described above reflect these concerns and, though there is still much to be done in terms of the detailed planning for implementation, they bode well for the future. Though resources for education, including trained personnel, are meagre and insufficient and problems abound, it is to be hoped that the same sacrifice, perseverance, and discipline that eventually won the war against a militarily much stronger enemy can be used to build lasting education for democracy in Eritrea.

9

Namibia: from Oppression and Resistance to Education for Democracy

Namibia achieved independence in 1990 after one hundred years of colonisation and a thirty-year war of liberation from the South African apartheid regime. The new government has not only set about ensuring greater access to education for African students but has also introduced a new and democratic philosophy of what it terms 'learner centred education'. The following quotation, for example, is a powerful statement about the connection between education and democracy, and comes from a book published by the Ministry of Education and Culture in Windhoek. The book has a supporting foreword from both the President, Sam Nujoma, and the then Minister of Education and Culture, Nahas Angula:

> To develop education for democracy we must develop democratic education . . . Our learners must study how democratic societies operate and the obligations and rights of their citizens. Our learners must understand that democracy means more than voting . . . [and] . . . that they cannot simply receive democracy from those who rule their society. Instead they must build, nurture and protect it. And they must learn that they can never take it for granted. In the past we were fooled by an authoritarian government that preached to us about democracy. Nor will learners today be deceived by an education system that talks about democracy and says it is for someone else at some other time. To teach about democracy our teachers – and our education system as a whole – must practice democracy. (Ministry of Education and Culture, 1993a: 41)

This chapter is based on interviews and documentation gathered during visits to Namibia in 1992, 1993, 1994 and 1996. It explores the political development of education in Namibia from the colonial period to the present day and discusses policies which attempt to implement democratic education in an independent Namibia.

A Brief History of Namibia

South West Africa (Namibia) became a German colony in 1890, though there was considerable resistance; in particular, the years 1904–7 were a period of continual rebellion. Namibia ceased being a German colony as a result of the First World War. Soldiers of the Union of South Africa marched into Windhoek in 1915 and in 1920 South Africa was given the mandate of trusteeship for Namibia by the League of Nations. This meant that South Africa, under a mandate to the British Crown, administered the territory as 'a sacred trust of civilisation'. However, in 1948 the Afrikaner National Party came to power in South Africa and refused to recognise the United Nations as the legal successor to the League. In practice, therefore, Namibia became a fifth province of South Africa and the racist political and economic system of apartheid was gradually introduced. In 1966 the UN formally revoked the mandate and in 1971 the International Court of Justice ruled that the South African occupation of Namibia was illegal.

Mass, organised resistance by Namibians began in the late 1950s during the height of the success of the nationalist movements in the ex-British and French African colonies. The first mass organisation was the Ovamboland Peoples' Organisation formed in 1958 among Namibia's largest ethnic group but in 1960 this developed into the South West African People's Organisation (SWAPO). As its origins suggest, SWAPO initially recruited predominantly from northern Ovambo speakers. However, focusing their opposition on the near slavery of the contract labour system, whereby African workers became virtually the property of those for whom they worked, SWAPO was able to organise in almost all parts of Namibia. In the early 1960s SWAPO was committed to a policy of non-violent reform but South Africa's determined and continued implementation of apartheid and the regular arrest, detention and torture of SWAPO members led to a change of policy. In 1966 a base of the People's Liberation Army of Namibia (PLAN), the military wing of SWAPO, was attacked at a camp at Omgulumbashe which signalled the beginning of a war that would last until 1989 (Brown, 1995: 19).

Colonial Education to 1948

The education system of pre-colonial Namibia was similar to that found elsewhere in Africa, being an integral part of everyday life rather than a specialist activity carried out in particular buildings. Knowledge, skills, values and roles were learned from parents and other adults by, for example, conversation, imitation, stories, games, song and ceremonies. The arrival of the German colonialists changed matters only slowly.

The German authorities introduced organised education for the white settler population in 1909 but they provided no education for the Namibian population as at this stage they did not consider it necessary for the economic development of the territory. Indeed, there was always the risk that education would implant 'undesirable ideas such as democracy and equality' (Salia-Bao, 1991: 15). The missionaries, on the other hand, saw schools as a way of creating Christian communities and they established a few primary schools in small scattered communities throughout the country from the late nineteenth century onwards.

With this desire to spread Christianity, however, came the belief that European civilisation based on Christianity was superior to African civilisation and thus missionary schools also set out to impart Western culture. Key aims of missionary education were therefore to 'tame' Africans to become both servile and to despise their own culture and history. As Christian educated Africans would also take part in the economy of the communities attached to the new mission stations they would need sufficient schooling to become efficient employees, but no more. As one missionary put it:

> For its development . . . the country does not need 'educated negroes', but competent, intelligent workers. The main emphasis will therefore be on education for obedience, order, punctuality, sobriety, honesty, diligence and moderation rather than academic learning. (Ellis, 1984: 14)

The South African administration between the First World War and the election of the Nationalists in 1948 was more interested in controlling missionary education to ensure its minimalist nature than in providing education for the African population itself. Contrary to education for whites, which was made compulsory between the ages of 7 and 17 as early as 1921, the total number of primary schools built for Africans from the beginning of the South African mandate up to 1940 was two, both in the central region of the country. Not one state school was built in northern Namibia, where the majority of the African population lived. White South African settlers during this period saw education for Africans as dangerous. As one put it:

> to educate them is to give them contact with world movements and world thinking which, of course, . . . inculcates such mischievous and intolerable ideas as democracy, the brotherhood of man, fundamental human freedoms, and the like. (quoted in Katjavivi, 1988: 27)

The Introduction of Apartheid Education

The election of the Nationalist Party in South Africa in 1948 marked the beginning of a change in educational policy both in South Africa and subsequently in Namibia. In 1945 one prominent member of the Nationalist Party declared in the House of Assembly:

> As has been correctly stated here, education is the key to the creation of the proper relationship between Europeans and non-Europeans in South Africa . . . Put native education on a sound basis and half the racial questions are solved . . . I say that there should be reform of the whole educational system and it must be the culture and background and the whole life of the native himself in his tribe . . . This whole (present) policy is also a danger for our own Western civilisation. (quoted in O'Callaghan, 1977: 99)

In 1949 the Eiselen Commission was set up and it reported in 1951. The report and the Bantu Education Act of 1953 formed the basis of the education system for South Africa which was later extended to Namibia. The state would now increase the provision of schooling for Africans as the growing economy required many more literate blacks but such education would be separate, unequal and aimed at ideological control. In 1954, H. F. Verwoerd, the Minister for Native Affairs and a leading architect of apartheid and Bantu education, stated that:

> The Bantu must be guided to serve his own community in all respects. There is no place for him in the European community above the level of certain forms of labour . . . For that reason it is of no avail for him to receive a training which has as its aim absorption in the European community, where he cannot be absorbed. (Nyaggah, 1980: 69)

The apartheid system of education was based on the philosophy of Christian National Education. Education should, according to CNE, inculcate in the white population the aspiration to guard its identity for 'God had willed separate nations and peoples, giving each nation and people its special calling, tasks and gifts' (O'Callaghan, 1977: 99). Education for blacks, on the other hand, should be in mother tongue, should not be funded at the expense of education for whites; should not prepare blacks for equal participation in society; should preserve the 'cultural identity' of the black communities while persuading them to accept Christian National principles and must, of necessity, be administered by whites. Enslin (1984: 140–1) notes the apparent contradiction between the relativist view which sees each group as having its own cultural identity and beliefs about education, and the argument that Afrikaaners have a special responsibility as trustees of black education. This, he argues, is an expression of the ideology of racial superiority of whites. Black africans, in their state of 'cultural infancy', learn in schools of their need for the guidance of the superior white culture. Black children are thus to learn submission to the rules of the established order.

In 1958 the Van Zyl Commission was appointed to set up and introduce a system based on this philosophy into Namibia. There were essentially three parts to the plan which was to determine the structure of education in Namibia up to independence. First, there would be an expansion of provision of black education so that by 1988 80 per cent of black children would have a basic four years of primary education. Second, black education was to be moved from the missionaries to the state, partly because of the need to resource the planned expansion but also because the churches could no longer be trusted to transmit apartheid ideology correctly. Third, education beyond the lower primary level was to be severely restricted. Only 20 per cent would go on to higher primary school and only one secondary school would be provided for each ethnic group. Initially, the education system was administered by South Africa along 'racial' lines with different systems for white, black 'coloureds' ('mixed race'). In 1980, however, eleven separate education authorities were set up to administer education on ethnic lines.

Apartheid Education in Practice

Although separate, educational provision in Namibia was not equal. For whites education was compulsory and paid for from tax whereas blacks always had to pay directly for their education in the form of fees. Given that wealth was concentrated in white hands and that 93 per cent of all personal income tax is paid by whites it is not surprising that in 1981, for example, per capita expenditure on black pupils was 232 Rand, 300 for 'coloureds' and 1210 for whites (Ellis, 1984: 41).

The content and processes of apartheid education in colonial Namibia were also aimed at perpetuating inequality. As Sam Nujoma, now President of Namibia, put it: 'Bantu education is simply brain-washing the African to believe that he's inferior – to prepare him for a life of labouring for the white "baas"' (Leu, 1980: 153). Ellis provides examples of text and illustrations from textbooks that reflect various themes of the ideology of apartheid. Images used in the textbooks reinforce a perception of whites as peaceful, resourceful and courageous and of blacks as war-like and ungrateful. A Eurocentric and fundamentalist Christian view of whites as the carriers of civilisation is given. Training for citizenship inculcates a sense of civilisation under siege from 'communism and terrorism'. Southern Africa is represented as a multi-racial society but blacks are presented as anthropological curiosities (1984: 16, 22, 42, 46).

The role of African teachers in the colonial education system was difficult and contradictory. On the one hand, they were the employees of the South African government which expected them to transmit the ideology of apartheid. Indeed, as one Namibian writer notes, there were strong pressures for acquiescence because their salaries were paid by the state. They knew that their housing bonds were heavily subsidised, if not entirely subsidised by government and that their cars needed to be changed every two years (Chase, 1987: 145).

On the other hand, many teachers did not like the syllabus and had to make it known to their communities that they disapproved of the government which paid their salaries at the risk of possible dismissal or even detention by the security forces. John Ya-Otto, a leading member of SWAPO and himself a teacher during the 1960s, describes this contradiction clearly:

> Katjimune's school must have given the school board constant head-aches, because they frequently sent us inspectors who would appear in the classroom without any warning. The inspectors were looking for us teachers to slip up, for some pretext to fire us. To them our school was a SWAPO nest, a hotbed of subversive ideas. They were right, of course, but I was always careful that my students were ahead in all their subjects before I talked about politics . . . It was often difficult to separate our dual roles. Our country's history is one of oppression, and no person of conscience could teach that history as the South African texts presented it. Nor could we ignore our students' questions about independence in other African countries and how we could win ours. (Ya-Otto, 1982: 63–4)

Perhaps even more worrying for the longer term future of education in Namibia were the classroom methods used. In the mid-1980s the classroom environment was still essentially authoritarian:

> Children are expected to be well behaved sponges, absorbing the text-book knowledge relayed by the teachers and furthermore to reproduce these facts in examinations. It is not part of the educational philosophy to train these pupils to think by themselves nor to question the teachers. (Chase, 1986: 51)

s and with staff
ioning (Cleaver
e schools were
' South Africa's

aching methods
ne Bantu educa-
still resembled
detail in chapter
deposited' in the
apitalize' (Freire
ching where the
front of the class
t and repeat it in

acher produces
k. The students
ce the material.
. In discussion
assion, nothing
kes place since
n the textbook

ce Forces (SADF)
AN – SWAPO's
) and inevitably
SADF was that
er cent military.
s' campaign that
ough developing
thereby creating
el therefore took
als and teaching.
rs as teachers can

nistake, or if he
ding you that he

' failed was that at

Resistance

ils became a regular feature of
the International Court of Justice
ing occupation of Namibia was
hools throughout Namibia but
that militancy was particularly
st 1971, when the Minister of
gwediva Training College, the
y 10 August a full-scale student
ely. Ignoring the opposition of
he authorities expelled those it
nts in Soweto in South Africa
n Namibia. Beginning with a
t Martin Luther High School
ts throughout the country had
sponded quickly and harshly
ken in for questioning. Teach-
. The Nama teachers strike of
ted by local communities and
epresented over 1,000 teachers
279–80).
e schools opened in Namibia;
neid education. One survey of
schools of resistance', in 1988
d introduced English as the
d introduced the curriculum
, others had kept the South
at it is doubtful whether the
iculum really constituted an
hool, for example, although
ere contrasted with the 'true
memorise apartheid history

ntolerable challenge to the
e assumption of black infe-
t many of the teachers were
nvolved in direct political
ative school at Koichas, for
he present government and
his puppets. So by the time
gh level of understanding.'
d to regular repression and

harassment with police and army making regular visi
and students being taken to the police station for ques
and Wallace, 1990: 72–3). But the mere fact that the
allowed to exist at all in the late 1980s was a sign c
loosening grip on the country.

Nevertheless, because of the examinations and the t
experienced by the teachers themselves as victims of
tion system, even in these schools classroom metho
Paulo Freire's 'banking method', discussed in more
3, whereby knowledge (as defined by the teacher) is
student and on which he or she is later expected to 'c
1972). It is marked by traditional, didactic forms of te
teacher formally transmits factual knowledge from the
and where the learners passively receive it, memorise
examinations. Thus at the alternative schools:

> instruction is a one-way process for the teachers. The t
> the material exactly according to the prescribed textboc
> are reduced to objects of instruction who have to reprod
> Whether they understand it or not is secondary . .
> subjects such as literature or history there is no disc
> is called into question, no training in critical thinking
> neither teacher nor students know what it is. What is
> is sacrosanct. (Helbig, 1989: 27–8)

Education and War

The liberation war between the South African Defer
and the Peoples' Liberation Army of Namibia (PI
military wing) took place between 1966 and 198
affected education. One oft-quoted premise of the
the war was 80 per cent political and only 20
On this premise was based the 'hearts and mind
aimed to gain control of the local population th
public works, improving the quality of life and
dependence on military structures. SADF person
over key posts in the public services such as hosp
The counter-productive nature of this policy of soldi
be gauged from one Namibian woman's reaction:

> Imagine somebody teaching you and if you make a
> suspects you, he would just point his gun at you, te
> would shoot you or your mother. (Konig, 1983: 31)

Part of the reason why the hearts and minds polic

the same time the SADF pursued a contradictory policy of terrorising the local population, including those at school. Particularly notorious were the Koevoet, a counter-insurgency unit infamous for its terror tactics. Violence against school pupils was widespread and commonplace:

> Army and Koevoet bases were positioned within shelling range of secondary schools. When attacked by the guerillas, they would vent their fury on their neighbours, lobbing shells indiscriminately into classrooms and hostels. Or Koevoet might put on a 'body display' as they did for pupils in the playground of Outapi secondary school, driving with the corpses of guerrillas strapped to the Casspirs (tanks). Drunken soldiers and Koevoet frequently broke into school dormitories to rape schoolgirls. Once, disguised as guerrillas, they kidnapped boarders, released them the following day in Angola, then arrested teachers and the Namibian National Student Organisation (NANSO) leaders for not reporting the incident! . . . The gun leaning in the classroom corner, bases looming over the playground, moronic syllabuses, money flung away on a divided and corrupt educational system, were certain proof that apartheid education offered the youth of Namibia nothing but servitude. Its only merit was that it quickened the will to resist. (Herbstein and Evensen, 1989: 117, 121)

Resistance by school pupils took a number of forms. One was strikes and boycotts. A second response to the intolerable educational conditions was to go into exile. This exodus was given an extra impetus by the introduction of compulsory military service for all male youths between the ages of 16 and 25 in 1981. Pupils therefore became prime targets for recruitment. Some exiles went to schools in Cuba and East Germany while others were sent for education elsewhere in Africa. However, the majority remained in SWAPO refugee camps in two countries close to Namibia – Angola and Zambia.

Two refugee camps, the SWAPO health and education centres at Nyango (Zambia) and Kwanza Sul (Angola), were particularly important in supplying Namibian refugees with education. Such education emphasised literacy and a non-South African version of Namibian history, with English being used as the medium of instruction. However, political education inevitably formed a significant part of the educational programme:

> we do not beautify war as a purpose or regard it as a form of sport. We see war for what it is – an extension of politics by other means. It is politics which leads the gun. SWAPO freedom fighters are, first and foremost, armed political militants. It is the duty of each and every cadre, wherever he or she goes, to explain the aims and objectives of SWAPO so that people know why their sons and daughters are armed and fighting the enemy, why they are prepared to sacrifice their lives for the freedom of their country. (SWAPO, 1981: 262)

These lessons in ideology were intended to reinforce motivation for those faced with a well-armed and numerically superior stand-ing army. It was also a preparation for another important function of a freedom fighter, to make contact with the people back home and keep them informed about the aims and successes of the war. However, the degree of success of such political education must be questioned on two grounds. First, although the tone of SWAPO's official ideology was officially socialist from 1976, there was in fact a lack of overall ideological coherence. SWAPO was very concerned about getting international support from a diverse range of countries for a primarily nationalist struggle for independence and therefore it had to be pragmatic and its rhetoric had to match its audience. A close examination of SWAPO's official documents from 1960 reveals that ideology was inconsistent and eclectic (Dobell, 1995). Maintaining a coherent and consistent line in political education classes would therefore be difficult.

A second problem was that the structures and political culture of SWAPO tended to be predominantly authoritarian in nature and 'no questions' was a repeated theme of the war. This problem has been analysed in detail and by Leys and Saul (1995) using interviews with many SWAPO personnel. Factors such as sustained military insecurity in the face of a more powerful enemy, divisions in the ranks based on ethnicity, age and region, the pressures of handling large numbers of refugees and the influence of Eastern European single party, 'vanguard' style socialism led to a situation where:

> In exile, the (SWAPO) leadership developed a political culture that frowned on spontaneity and debate, increasingly defined criticism as disloyalty, and eventually gave free rein to those in charge of the movement's 'security'. (Leys and Saul, 19–95: 5)

This seems to have influenced the style of political education which was formal, abstract and one way:

> Little has been written concerning the nature of political education that took place in the SWAPO camps, usually led by political commissars trained on scholarships in China, the USSR and in Eastern European countries. The evidence suggests, however, that rote learning rather than critical thinking was emphasised in such instruction . . . (Dobell, 1995: 175)

Teachers in the SWAPO camps, at least until the mid-1980s, tended to reproduce the attitudes and patterns of behaviour of the colonial system and pupils found it difficult to overcome the authoritarian modes of reception they had been conditioned to obey:

> Receptive and repetitive patterns of learning predominate over creative ones. If teaching in SWAPO education centres is to present a true

alternative to the colonial system, if it is not to reduce itself to merely substituting one set of political data for another, then the compilation and writing of teaching material must be oriented toward more emancipatory modes of education. Only if it does can the forms of human communication and authoritarian relationships established under colonialism be replaced and only then can a more humane society be built and preserved. (Gatter, 1987: 31)

Yet it would be surprising if the commitment to democratic education which clearly existed at independence, as will be discussed below, had no origins and precedents whatsoever in the independence struggle. Leys and Saul end their study of the liberation struggle in Namibia with the following words:

> For the liberation struggle developed strength and resilience in SWAPO and a tradition of challenge to authority, as well as one of hierarchy and authoritarianism. All we can say is that what prevailed during the struggle was the latter tradition . . . (1995: 203)

The key word here is 'prevailed' as there certainly were democratic counter currents. As Leys and Saul also make clear, one source of pressure for greater democracy in the liberation struggle was students and the more educated, particularly those who had studied in South Africa at the time of mass resistance in the townships in the mid-1970s. The seeds of this concern for greater democracy in education grew gradually out of a rejection of the nature of apartheid 'Bantu' education which as well as being racist was essentially authoritarian. Therefore, although a political culture of authoritarianism might have prevailed in SWAPO and the liberation struggle, education was one area where democracy and participation began to be debated and practised in the decade before independence in 1990. There were trends in this direction in the liberation movement both inside and outside Namibia.

Inside Namibia, the Namibian National Student Organisation (NANSO), which was formed in June 1984, had as one of its initial objectives the replacement of the prefect system in schools with democratically elected Student Representative Councils. The purposes of the SRCs were:

- to coordinate all the student activities at school and represent the students wherever possible;
- to act as a mediator between students and the school authority, the public and community organisations;
- to provide the necessary direction for student activities and ensure the link between parents and student;
- to draft a constitution as a guiding force for its activities;

- to be politically active, responsible, and clear on its objectives; and

- to educate and assist students by organising workshops and seminars.

By 1987–8 there were, for example, SRCs in most secondary schools on Ovamboland (Amukugo, 1993: ch. 5).

Although, as described above, many of the alternative schools founded in opposition to apartheid tended to reproduce some of its authoritarian characteristics, the People's Primary School which was founded in Katatura in 1986 seems to have been something of an exception. At this school greater emphasis was placed on critical thinking and self-expression as the basic aim of education. Teachers were encouraged to assist the children in developing a positive self-image, self-confidence and initiative, as well as a creative mind. Corporal punishment was forbidden and a system of parental involvement in the school's activities was introduced. Evening classes for parents were introduced and covered, for example, non-authoritarian relationships with children, alternative modes of punishment, the learning and study environment at home, how to assist children with school work and health issues (Amukugo, 1993: 108–10).

Outside Namibia, the term 'democratisation' in SWAPO work on education stemming from Zambia in the early 1980s is used in terms of equal access to education rather than the processes of education. Also, given the broadly socialist orientation of SWAPO at the time, there is an interest in education with production as espoused in education for self-reliance in Tanzania (Angula, 1982; Tjitendero, 1982, 1984).

However, by the mid-1980s there were signs that SWAPO thinking on education was moving in a more democratic direction. The Namibia Secondary Technical School, which was funded by the Norwegian government, was opened in Loudima, Congo in December 1986. This was established by SWAPO as a pilot school to try out new ideas for secondary education in an independent Namibia. Its curricular approach was influenced both by the presence of Scandinavian teachers and advisers and SWAPO's desire to begin to work in a way that was the antithesis of the South African style of education dominant in the then South West Africa. The South African matriculation examination was therefore rejected as politically and educationally unacceptable as it depended on rote learning and repetition of content instead of encouraging creative and critical thinking. Instead, the more skills based International General Certificate of Secondary Education was chosen and there was an emphasis on pre-vocational skills and education with production.

After independence students from the Loudima school were moved to Mweshipandeka Secondary School in northern Namibia. An evaluation of this move (Brock-Utne, Appiah-Endresen and Oliver, 1994) demonstrates the difference between the ethos of the Loudima School and a 'normal' school in Namibia. The existing students at Mweshipandeka found it difficult to get used to the Loudima students. The latter, used to a learner centred curriculum that used group work, discussion and critical thinking and which encouraged them to challenge the teachers, were seen by the former as rude and lacking in respect as they were more ingrained with such African values as showing respect to elders and not disagreeing publically with someone senior in age. While some of the Namibian teachers shared similar feelings and were sceptical about the new approach to learning, others said they loved to teach these students because they were so interested in learning, so active and so challenging. One teacher said 'I wish all students could have been like these students' (p. 17).

In Mweshipandeka the educational model that had been tried out at Loudima was introduced for all pupils in 1992. There was, understandably, some resistance to this from the school's longer serving teachers, particularly as the new subjects and teaching methods meant a longer day with no extra pay. Nevertheless, the evaluators were definite about the impact that the Loudima experience had had on the school:

> Our classroom observations leave no doubt that positive changes in the learning situation have taken place. We found no classrooms of the traditional type where desks are arranged in rows all facing the teacher. In all classrooms desks were arranged for group work and students were actively working in groups or pairs. They were conducting experiments and had an open and friendly relationship to teachers and also to us. (p. 23)

While Loudima was perhaps the most important educational model for an independent Namibia, the SWAPO education centre at Kwanza-Sul in Angola also experienced change in the same direction during the period 1980–9. The head of the centre from 1985 identified two key sources of influence. First, Namibian teachers returning from Teaching English as a Foreign Language courses in Britain in 1984 who were keen to introduce new teaching methods and second the Integrated Teachers Training Programme run by Swedish teacher educators. These influenced teaching so that by 1989 it had become more child centred (interview with Joseph Mangopo, 10 August 1994). Also, students were represented on the School Committee via the SWAPO Youth League (SWAPO of Namibia, Department of Education and Culture 1988).

Education Since Independence

On the eve of Namibian independence in 1989 global politics had changed significantly from the international context which had existed during most of SWAPO's liberation struggle. Communism had collapsed in Eastern Europe and democracy had become dominant internationally and the political model for the new Namibia. Moreover, it was clear that education was to play a role in this. At a conference on teacher education in Namibia held in Zambia in September 1989 Nahas Angula, soon to be Namibia's first independent Minister of Education and Culture, stated:

> Education in independent Namibia will both a challenge and an opportunity to all those who cherish the ideals of a truly free, democratic and just society. Education will be a challenge because it is expected to contribute to the integration and democratisation of society. It is equally expected to enhance equality, social justice, mutual understanding and national reconciliation. (United Nations Institute for Namibia, 1989: 15)

A major consultancy on education published as Namibia became independent (Turner 1990) pointed out some of the major changes that needed to be made to the inherited system of education if education was to be compatible with these aims:

> It is clear that both the curriculum and the examinations system need to be re-modelled. The present system is oriented towards rote learning and carrying out instructions . . . Social sciences are also of the greatest importance if the future citizens of the country are to understand the place of Namibia not only in Southern Africa but also in a world context. It is important, in developing the new curriculum, that full attention is given not just to subject content but to the whole style of teaching which is adopted. The present common practice of virtually lecturing to bored and uncomprehending groups of students must be avoided. Instead, wherever possible, the pupils should learn through activity, through projects and through individual guided study as well as by co-operative group activity . . . The change of emphasis from rote learning to understanding, from inactive to activity methods, from individual to group activity, will require a total reorientation on the part of the teachers. (pp. 34, 86, 113)

The gap between the desires of the new SWAPO government and the reality on the ground was made clear at an important conference on basic education held in Etosha in April 1991 (Snyder, 1991). The President, Sam Nujoma, spoke of the need for learner-centred education to develop the skills necessary for responsible citizenship. He stated:

> The special emphasis that I believe is guiding deliberations in this conference is that education must be child- or learner-centred. The

Namibian basic education must support the actual processes of individual learning, rather than continue the colonial teacher-centred Bantu
education, with an emphasis on control, rigid discipline, parrot-like
learning and negative assessment principles. (p. 5)

Reports from inspectors and teachers, however, drew attention to the
obstacles facing such change noting that there was too much emphasis
on passing traditional examinations based on memorisation and that
therefore rote learning was used as the mainstay in the majority of
classes and subjects, that corporal punishment was still the order
of the day in many primary schools; and that authoritarianism and
dependency were the most common features of school organisation
and management. A Ministry survey of junior secondary schools in
September/October 1991confirmed that this was indeed the case with
student representative councils not functioning as efficiently as they
could and all but five of the 250 lessons observed uniformly teacher-
centred and non-participatory. It pointed to the need for changes in
teacher education, assessment, curriculum and teaching materials in
order to bring about more learner centred education. It also made
the important point that students shape classroom expectations as
well as teachers and that they also need to be acquainted with new
approaches for them to function (Ministry of Education and Culture,
1991a). Another piece of research carried out at this time and involving
330 randomly selected classes and teachers found that 91 per cent of the
teachers used a lecturer or chalk and talk method (Mkandawire, 1993:
143).

As a result of the Etosha conference the Ministry of Education noted
its annual report in December 1991 that:

a continuous, multi-dimensional process has been directed toward the
transformation of Namibian primary and junior secondary education.
From the social and pedagogical limitations characteristic of the inherited South African system, a wider range of measures have been applied
to implementing the letter and spirit of the Constitution as well as
transforming the Namibian classroom into an accessible, learner-centred
and effective learning environment. (Ministry of Education and Culture,
1991b: 10)

The remainder of this chapter will examine certain key aspects of the
educational reform process in Namibia – curriculum and assessment,
teacher education and school management.

Curriculum and Assessment

'We must understand quality even more broadly . . . consider a primary school where children master basic reading, writing and numbers but do not learn about citizenship in a democratic society or respect for others' culture and values. That is not high quality education' (Ministry of Education and Culture, 1993a: 39). The school curriculum has traditionally often been seen solely in technical terms of, for example, improving literacy and numeracy as though these are unproblematically value free and good things in their own right. The Namibian educational reforms, however, are informed by a philosophy which has asked more basic questions about the purposes of education. As a result literacy and numeracy are seen as necessary but not sufficient. The reasons for literacy and numeracy are part of more fundamental questions about the sort of human beings and the sort of society that are the ultimate purpose of education. Only when these basic value questions are answered can a curriculum be framed which meets those aims. Avoiding these questions and pretending that curriculum planning is in some way a neutral, value-free exercise is to ignore existing divisions and inequalities in society, such as those based on gender or 'race', and is likely to result in their reproduction.

In Namibia the answer to questions about the nature of society and individuals is in terms of a democratic and egalitarian society composed of individuals who share these values. The major goals of education are seen in terms of access, equity, quality and democracy. Some of the goals of Basic Education, for example, are to:

- promote national unity, justice and democracy;
- promote human rights, respect for oneself and respect for others, their cultures and their religious beliefs;
- foster the highest moral, ethical and spiritual values such as integrity, responsibility, equality and reverence for life;
- encourage perseverance, reliability, accountability and respect for the value and dignity of work; and
- develop literacy, numeracy, understanding of the natural and social environment, civic life, artistic appreciation and expression, social skills, and promote physical and mental health. (Ministry of Education and Culture, 1993a: 55)

The ideal democratic citizen, therefore, is somebody that not only possesses certain values but also certain skills or personality traits – they are critical, articulate, confident, creative and independent. This suggests that teaching and learning which encourages openness, discussion, doubt, exploration, choice, trust, respect, participation and problem-solving. The phrase that is used to describe this new approach in Namibia is 'learner-centred education'. Some of the features of learner-centred education (LCE) that emerged from a Ministry of Education sponsored workshop are as follows (each is further developed in an appendix):

1   Active student participation in learning.
2   Conceptual learning beyond factual learning.
3   A willingness by teachers to let go of some of the old ideas.
4   An emphasis on problem-solving.
5   New technology, properly used, encourages LCE.
6   Continuous assessment of teaching and learning.
7   Accountability for the results of teaching and learning.
8   Learning integrated across subject areas.
9   An emphasis on the 'whole' learner.
10 Systematic use of valuable life experiences.
11 Sufficient curriculum time for teacher and student initiated activities.
12 Encouragement of creativity on the part of the learner.
13 Encouragement of trial and error learning.
14 Encouragement of choice.
15 Encouragement of both flexibility and balance – the teacher as guide or coach, not as expert.
16 All teachers and learners are both learners and teachers.
17 Peer teaching by students.
18 Stress on the joy of teaching and learning.
19 Patience on everyone's part.
20 Opportunity and time for small group instruction is encouraged in all classes.
21 Mutual respect and co-operation of all teachers and learners.
22 LCE is appropriate for all school subjects and all school levels.
23 LCE is appropriate for all students, regardless of ability level or sophistication.
24 LCE does not necessarily require a new curriculum.
25 Every student can be successful; there are no required failures.
26 Remedial teaching as necessary.
27 LCE requires both preparation and spontaneity.
28 Individualised instruction as resources permit.
29 LCE requires a high level of discipline and order. (Ministry of Education and Culture, 1993b: 81–6)

At the workshop on the training of trainers from which these features come, Patti Swartz of the Ministry of Education and Culture pointed to a number of misconceptions about learner-centred education. The first is that teachers relinquish control. However, this is not true as teachers still remain the authority in the subject or field but they facilitate the learning process without being authoritarian. A second is that LCE gives more time to the teacher but the teachers have to be better prepared for lessons as they have to be ready to change their style and approach to meet the needs of the learners and also to deal with issues that may arise on account of the learners being more active, critical, exploratory and enquiring. A third is that LCE waters down expected results as teachers no longer ask and answer all the questions; but what is not understood is that achievement through interactive participation, enquiry, the application of knowledge to real-life situations and problem-solving is more rewarding, more lasting and of more value. This constitutes true and effective learning as the learner remembers and retains the knowledge obtained in this way and will be able to utilise and apply the skills acquired in this way. A final misconception is that LCE leads to chaos, but if handled correctly learners become more motivated and more self-disciplined (Ministry of Education and Culture, 1993b: 16).

If learner-centred education is to be successfully introduced then assessment is an issue that must be confronted. In practice teachers often start with assessment and work backwards, i.e. their teaching is based on what they think will be assessed rather than their assessment being based on what they have decided to teach. Changing assessment is therefore a vital aspect of changing teaching and learning. A study at the time of independence, however, found that existing examination and assessment procedures did not match the new philosophy of education: 'The emphasis on failure is endemic throughout the education system with students expecting to fail, teachers expecting them to fail and examiners setting papers to ensure that they fail' (Bethell, 1990: 80). In contrast the Ministry of Education and Culture now espouses a very different viewpoint:

> Research on learning is quite clear. Rewards work better than pun-
> ishments. Success stimulates learning. Failure holds it back. Posi-
> tive reinforcement promotes more and more rapid learning. Negative
> reinforcement does just the opposite. Indeed, when the messages to
> students are largely negative and punitive, most will find school
> painful rather than exciting. many will simply stop trying. (Ministry
> of Education and Culture, 1993a: 126).

The Ministry of Education and Culture has therefore started to introduce criterion-based assessment at all levels. Existing traditional South African examinations have been replaced by the International General Certificate of Education and the Higher International General Certificate of Education at the Senior Secondary level. The principle behind these examinations is that students are rewarded for positive achievement – what they know, understand and can do – rather than being penalised for an accumulation of errors. IGCSE and HIGCSE use a wide range of assessment techniques appropriate for different skills and attributes in different subjects. These include oral and listening tests, practicals, project work, performance and course work as well as various types of written examination which can involve skills such as comprehension, analysis, synthesis and application as well as memorisation (Ministry of Education and Culture, 1993a: 123–8; Ministry of Education, 1993c: 1, 7).

If the democratic and egalitarian philosophy of education enshrined in learner-centred curriculum and assessment is to be successfully implemented it must also be reflected in teaching materials. A good example of the new type of textbook being introduced in Namibia is *Racing Ahead* (1994) which is an IGCSE book for English as a second language. The book has a Namibian and African focus and is balanced in terms of its portrayal of 'racial' groups and genders. Throughout each chapter are tasks which encourage independent learning and which develop skills of comprehension, self-expression and communication and co-operation. The publicity material for the book states that two of the aims of the book are:

> To encourage skills of critical thinking and argument. Learners need to be able to use the English language in order to express and support their opinions. But first they need to develop a critical attitude.
> To encourage critical awareness of contemporary issues such as gender, development and the environment.

One example among many of how this is achieved is from the chapter on tourism. In this chapter the students are asked to discuss and write down the advantages and disadvantages of tourism. However, and very importantly in terms of education for democracy, there is also guidance on the language and nature of discussion and debate. Students are asked to look as a series of words and phrases such as 'That's exactly what I think', 'Absolutely', 'I agree', 'I disagree', 'I couldn't agree with you more', 'I'm sorry, but I totally disagree', 'I'm not sure I agree with that', 'I think I'd go along with that', 'I'm sorry, but I just can't go along with that' and categorise them into which are the strongest and weakest ways of agreeing and disagreeing. Also, the students are asked to stage a debate on the benefits of tourism to Namibia and are referred to an earlier chapter which gives detailed information on how to organise a debate (*Racing Ahead*, 1994: 24–6, 68–9).

However, while learner-centred education can help to promote the values and skills of democracy across the curriculum, it is important that at some point in the curriculum learners are directly exposed to a more explicit form of political education for democracy. As was argued in chapter 5, one obvious curriculum area for this is social studies. The new social studies syllabus for primary education grades 4–7 in Namibia aims to do this in terms of knowledge, skills and attitudes. In terms of knowledge the content includes African and world history, civic groups and associations, traditional and modern government, national identity, constitutional guarantees, civic values, rights and responsibilities. Understanding of concepts is also stressed: these include, for example, social control, rule, law, democracy, leadership, power and authority, conflict, consensus and justice. Among the skills to be developed are critical thinking, creative thinking, decision making, problem solving and inquiry. The attitudes to be developed include:

- positive attitudes and critical tolerance towards other social, cultural and political values and beliefs, including appreciation of and confidence in oneself;
- commitment to human values such as justice, equality, truth, freedom, diversity and human rights;
- appreciation of our constitution and democratic behaviour;
- critical awareness of our society in order to become a truly democratic citizen;
- competence in making responsible judgements in terms of justice, equality and other democratic values. (Ministry of Education and Culture, 1994)

Teacher Education

Much is being asked of teachers in Namibia:

> The Namibian education system is undergoing a paradigm shift, a realignment of such dramatic proportions that its causative effects would most probably continue for many generations into the future. Quite suddenly our teachers are faced with a critical disjuncture in self-understanding. Their philosophical maps for teaching do not correlate any more with the changing social reality. (Hope, 1993: 126)

If classroom teaching is to change in Namibia then teacher education must also change in order to educate the new type of teachers that will be required. As noted above, an early model for a reformed teacher education was provided by the Swedish initiated Integrated Teacher Education Programme which existed at SWAPO's Education Centre in Kwanza-Sul, Angola between 1983 and 1989. One of the Swedish teacher educators involved noted that:

> We believe that there should be room in any given society for alternative models of teacher education founded on democratic principles . . . We have managed to create a different role of trainees which aims to foster self-reliant, active, creative, cooperative and committed teachers, who will be able to think and act independently and to utilize their own resources. (Dahlstrom et al., 1989: 81)

An influential report on teacher education sponsored by the Swedish International Development Agency (SIDA) and undertaken on behalf of the Ministry of Education and Culture shortly after independence (Andersson, Callewaert and Kallos, 1991) reaffirmed the need for change in this direction. It argued that the curriculum in Namibian schools was highly examination oriented, based on rote learning and favourable to a highly submissive pupil role in most parts of the country. To achieve a break with such a tradition required not only a new curriculum for schools but also new and more democratic forms of in-service and pre-service teacher education. This change was seen as particularly important in the context of a developing country where teachers are faced with shortages of teaching resources:

> A new system of teacher education must use a different pedagogical approach altogether. The new approach should enable the teacher candidates to work creatively, relying on and developing their own skills. The training programme must emphasise production and reflection rather than reproduction and rote learning. The teacher candidates must be trained to, and be prepared for, work in schools with insufficient material resources. (p. 28)

The argument for congruence between teacher training college and school is also strongly made in the report – if teachers are going to teach in a more active, participant and democratic manner in schools then they must actually experience these learning methods themselves on a regular basis in their own teacher education in college. However, the new teacher education must not only be participant it must also encourage a critical understanding of the social and economic context within which the school system operates, which implies an added weight placed on the sociology of education (pp. 66–7).

This philosophy is accepted by the Namibian government and reflected, for example, in the new Basic Education Teacher Diploma, which is a course for those who go on to teach in primary or junior secondary schools or those who have been teaching in such schools but who are as yet unqualified or under qualified. The democratic philosophy of this course is clear from its aims, of which the following are some:

Basic Teacher Education will strive to:

- develop a teacher who will respect and foster the values of our

Constitution, contribute to nation building, and respond positively to the changing needs of Namibia society;

- develop understanding and respect for diverse cultural values and
  beliefs;
- develop understanding and respect for human dignity, sensitivity,
  and commitment to the needs of learners;
- develop a reflective attitude and creative, analytical, and critical
  thinking;
- develop the ability to participate actively in collaborative decision
  making;
- promote gender awareness and equity to enable all Namibians to
  participate fully in all spheres of society;
- develop an understanding of learning as an interactive, shared
  and productive process;
- develop the ability to create learning opportunities which will
  enable learners to explore different ways of knowing and develop
  a whole range of their thinking abilities. (Ministry of Education
  and Culture, 1993a: 81–2)

The teaching on the new course is designed to be practical and
includes a wide variety of methods such as class visits, demonstra-
tion teaching, micro-teaching, team teaching, group work, individual
study, seminars, tutorials and lectures. Students should be encouraged
to form clubs and societies for co-curricular activities and to participate
in the democratic structures of the college together with staff. Assessment is intended to be consistent with the principles of learner-centred
education with an emphasis on what the student teachers know,
understand and can do, as the purpose is to provide conditions for
new teachers to succeed rather than to concentrate on weeding out
failures. A variety of continuous assessment techniques are therefore
to be used, such as essays, project work, teaching practice and a profile
of various pieces of practical work (Ministry of Education and Culture,
1993a, b).

Such radical changes to the nature of teacher education in Namibia
will not be easy to achieve. Patti Swartz of the Ministry of Education
and Culture expressed both the importance and the difficulty of this
task at a seminar for the teacher educators who will have to implement
the change:

> As pointed out by the Hon. Minister, it is not going to be an easy road
> on which we are just taking our first steps – it will sometimes demand
> much from us, sometime we will become anxious and frustrated;
> sometimes we might even feel like giving up – but in the end it
> will be worthwhile if we can produce self-reliant, productive, profes-
> sional, reflective, innovative, motivated teachers who will work towards

unifying the nation but who will respect cultural diversity . . . we are gathered here to depart from the old dispensation into the new one. (Ministry of Education and Culture, 1993d: 9–10)

At the same seminar Roger Avenstrup, an adviser to the Ministry, also pointed to the scale of the change when he argued that that the Basic Education Teacher programme was substantially different from previous approaches because it involved a different way of viewing knowledge itself as – 'the content of knowledge, the organisation of knowledge, the very concept of knowledge itself, is changing in the world around us. The old classifications and patterns of thought are not always adequate to understanding the rapidly changing modern world' (p. 10). However, a study of an in-service course for Namibian teachers (Rowell, 1995) suggests that, as might be expected, this view of knowledge as socially constructed rather than given or preordained is not currently prevalent. The teachers involved had a strong belief that there should be a pre-specified body of knowledge and/or skills which had been identified by the instructor. They saw knowledge as objective and independent of people and context. Having experienced the teacher-as-expert relationship for all of their school lives they needed considerable encouragement and time to begin looking at their personal beliefs about teaching and learning. They found it difficult to accord their personal knowledge the status of publicly accepted knowledge and had a view of knowledge as detached from the learner rather than a view of knowledge as constructed by the learner.

While existing teacher attitudes are undoubtedly a potential obstacle to reform, Rowell's view of the way to progress from this position is that the 'preconceptions held by future teachers of what it means to be a learner and what it means to be a teacher will have to be challenged by the very nature of the interactions in the teacher education program . . . ' (p. 12). This is the argument for congruence and consistency between practices in college and those desired in school made in chapter 7, which is indeed an integral part of the new Basic Teacher Education Diploma (BETD). Encouragingly, recent research on the Basic Education Teacher Diploma found that such consistency is improving. The research categorised teaching on the course into 'poor traditional' (15 per cent), 'poor progressive' (20 per cent), 'good traditional' (35 per cent) and 'good progressive' (30 per cent) so that traditional and progressive teaching was split 50/50. However, as the report comments:

a reasonable, informed guess (based on the interview results) is that there was very little of what is here labelled as 'progressive teaching' before the introduction of the BETD. Most of the teaching was fairly 'traditional' and, according to the interviews, quite a lot of it (maybe as much as 50%) would probably have been classified as 'poor'. From that perspective, the impact of the BETD is quite dramatic. In just a few years there has been a general move away from traditional to progressive teaching, and also from poor to good. (Frykholm, 1995: 58)

School Management

The nature of school management will also be a crucial factor in introducing and facilitating learner-centred education. Buddy Wentworth, the Deputy Minister for Education and Culture, speaking to a course for school inspectors, described the system of educational administration in the former South West Africa as follows:

> Most of us in this room share with one another a similar background of school management and educational administration. Whether in the most privileged schools or the most neglected schools, a common feature was the tight control, a sometimes rigid and inflexible dependence on top-down authority, the rigid authoritarianism of South African education philosophy. The net results of all this was that in the classrooms, the learners were clients and hostages to authoritarian, teacher-centred education and in the schools the teachers and principals were clients and hostages to the detailed control and attention of inspectors and subject advisers, who in turn were hostages and clients of the director who, whether knowingly or not, promoted the programmes of the authorities south of the Orange River. It was a perfect system for preventing change, for exercising a negative and punishing type of authority – a perfect system for telling people exactly what to do to stay out of trouble, how to be passive and avoid responsibility. (Ministry of Education and Culture, 1992a: Annex 4.5)

Buddy Wentworth went on to speak of the need to unlearn some of the old attitudes and practices such as thinking of authority as a permanent vertical structure rather than a two-way, horizontal process; refusing to ask for opinions and suggestions from the grass-roots level; telling teachers and principals exactly what to do to the smallest detail; trying to find fault rather than trying to help; expecting failure and jealously guarding one's authority rather than sharing it. Indeed, a report for USAID on Namiba noted that one of the accomplishments of the Namibian government since independence had been widespread access to, and participation in, various decision-making processes. It commented that field visits had indicated that this was a common conclusion with respect to inspectors, subject advisers and heads. The basic curriculum framework development process had also involved many groups from outside the Ministry structure such as churches, parents and NGOs in an extensive consultative process (USAID, 1993b: 7).

In terms of school management headteachers will play a vital role in achieving the learner-centred school. As the USAID report put it: 'School principals, using the appropriate skills and management styles, can be the best conduits for instilling democratic values in both learners and teachers' (USAID, 1993b: 54). A 'Training the Trainers' workshop held in 1993 for those who would go on to train primary school principals had as its main theme 'Managing the learner-centred school'. Participants at the workshop agreed that principals should not be unaccountable despots and that they should be aware of the desired hidden curriculum in a learner-centred school. The principal's responsibility was seen as being an example of well-mannered treatment of all persons without dominance or subservience, of setting an example of willingness to listen to others, to resolve differences of opinion amiably, to show fairness to all learners without favouritism and to show proper professional conduct towards teachers and learners (Ministry of Education and Culture, 1993b: 164–5). On another occasion the Deputy Permanent Secretary at the Ministry of Education and Culture noted that headteachers in the learner-centred school should exhibit empathy, respect and warmth, genuineness and clarity and should operate according to four management principles – participation, communication, recognition and delegated authority (1992b: 71).

The role of students in school management is described in the User's Guide to the Education Code of Conduct (1993) which has been agreed to by both student and teacher organisations. At grades 11 and 12 (sixth-form level) students are directly represented through democratic election on School Boards along with parents and teachers. School Boards have responsibility for such important matters as discipline, budgets, appointing teachers, the use of school facilities and school fees. At this level, therefore, students are fully involved in the democratic organisation of the schools. Below this level, however, their role is better described as consultative rather than democratic. They have the right to have their opinions considered on matters regarding discipline, rules and punishment but seem to have no formal role in actual decision making. Constructive student involvement in school decision making is, however, quite feasible at the pre-sixth form level (Harber, 1995: chs 2 and 3) and is an area where democratic school organisation could be further developed in Namibia in the future.

In April 1991 the Namibian Supreme Court ruled that corporal punishment was unconstitutional and since then the Namibian government has banned its use in schools and has published a booklet on alternatives to corporal punishment called 'Discipline From Within' (Ministry of Education and Culture, 1992c). Corporal punishment is one feature of authoritarianism and oppression that has been common in the management of African schools and is rightly seen as fundamentally inconsistent with learner-centred education for democracy because it humiliates learners, results in anger and resentment, removes co-operation, leads to an atmosphere of violence and is of no long-term value (Ministry of Education and Culture, 1993a: 132–3). Nevertheless, the Ministry has implemented this policy despite evidence that support for this form of punishment is still culturally ingrained. In one survey (Zimba, Auala and Scott, 1994) more than 50 per cent of students, 70 per cent of the parents and 80 per cent of the teachers indicated that they supported the use of corporal punishment in schools.

Conclusion

In May 1993 the American President Bill Clinton described Namibia as a model for democracy in sub-Saharan Africa. The Namibian government has recognised, however, that the survival of democracy cannot be taken for granted. It is important actively to promote and protect democracy and human rights. One mechanism for this is the education system where the new philosophy of learner-centred education has as one of its main aims the promotion of democratic values and behaviour. The implementation of this new policy will not be easy. The survey of attitudes to corporal punishment cited above indicates that many of the aspects of learner-centred education are new and unfamiliar to the Namibian population and in the short run are likely to face cultural resistance. Moreover, there are also severe practical problems such as inherited inequalities, shortage of trained teachers and heads, lack of sufficient funds and lack of proficiency in English, the new national language. Nevertheless, reform of this fundamental nature cannot afford to be piecemeal and the Namibian government has developed a broad and coherent educational policy and has embarked on reform on a number of complementary fronts at the same time. The building of a democratic political culture in Namibia will be a difficult task and will not happen overnight, but since independence in 1990 there has been a clear sense of purpose and direction. It is an important model of democratic educational innovation that should be observed closely by other countries in Africa and elsewhere.

10

Angels and Saints: Education for Democracy in the New South Africa

Education in South Africa has until recently been shaped by the racist philosophy of apartheid and has been characterised by racial inequality in terms of spending on education, access to education and the content of education (see, for example, Kallaway 1984). The nature of apartheid education is discussed in some detail in relation to Namibia in the previous chapter. However, the first ever democratic election in South Africa in 1994 resulted in a government led by the African National Congress (ANC) which is committed not only to racial equality in education but also to democratic forms of school management and curriculum, which will be essential in creating a culture in schools and the wider society based on human rights and mutual respect. In South Africa this will require what is often referred to as a 'radical paradigm shift' as schooling has been traditionally characterised not only by racism but also by an authoritarianism designed to encourage conformity and suppress a critical or questioning attitude in order to control a population confronted by patently unfair and unequal social structures. Given the theme of the present book, this chapter focuses primarily therefore not so much on racism in South African schools but rather on the closely related theme of power relations in schools and particularly on the role of students in their own education.

Authoritarianism in South African Education

Christie (1991: 146) argues that in terms of their overall organisation South African schools are essentially authoritarian institutions:

> If you go into any school – white or black – you'll soon know who is in charge. There is a ladder of seniority, with the principal

at the top, then deputy principals and vice principals, then senior teachers, then ordinary staff. You can even tell this hierarchy from the position and size of their offices and where they sit in the staffroom! Somewhere at the bottom of the hierarchy are the students. But even amongst students there is a hierarchy as well – prefects, senior students etc.

She goes on to argue that this authoritarianism is reflected in class-rooms where the teacher usually stands up front while the students sit passively at their desks. The students' role is to listen to and memorise what the teacher says. The students are not active, they simply receive the knowledge which the teachers transmit to their minds. As a result most students are not given an opportunity to think for themselves or to discover things for themselves and they don't develop a critical awareness of the world (1991: 168).

The following imaginary scene from a recent textbook on the sociol-ogy of education in South Africa captures such classroom relationships well:

Now class I want you to copy those notes from the board. Remember, you may not say a word to one another until the bell rings. After you have copied the notes I want you to memorise all the underlined facts for the test tomorrow. Anyone who fails the test will be punished. Now be quiet and start writing!'

Ten minutes into the lesson two pupils are seen whispering. 'Joseph, are you disobeying my instructions? Why do I always have to scream and beat you before you listen? What are those things on the side of your head – ornaments?'

No, Misss, I-I-I . . . '

'And you, Nomsa, do you need a hiding to help you concentrate better?'

'No Miss (blinking back the tears of fear). I just asked Joseph if I could borrow his pen, mine won't write'.

'Did I, or did I not, say that I will not have any talking?'

'You did, but Miss, my pen wouldn't . . . '

'Joseph, you will be given six of the best. Nomsa, I want you to copy Chapter 10 from your textbook, twice, by tomorrow . . . '

The authors comment that research in South Africa shows that similar undignified incidents are still common experiences for students today (McKay and Romm, 1995: 100). At a conference on science and maths education held in 1995 at the University of Natal, the conference brochure used a quote from a student to illustrate the general benefits of computers in South African schools, but the quote has other implications:

The computer never gets mad at me. I can make the same mistake ten times in a row and it doesn't tell me I am stupid or yell at me, or things like that. It just tells me I'm wrong, that I goofed, and asks me if I want to read that part again . . . not like my teacher. (Centre for the Advancement of Science and Maths Education, 1995: 11)

Indicative of the authoritarian nature of South African schools has been the widespread use of corporal punishment. One survey of 300 first-year university students found that 89 per cent reported that they had been physically punished at some stage during their school career (cited in Holdstock, 1990: 347). This problem has not yet disappeared. Recently human rights lawyers in KwaZulu Natal have threatened court action against some schools following incidents of indiscriminate beatings of students (*Sunday Tribune*, 6 August 1995). Reflecting on the damage done by corporal punishment both in terms of sanctioning and reproducing the use of violence, and in creating a climate of fear in which learning and achievement is discouraged, Holdstock gets to the educational heart of the matter when he comments that 'We need to rethink our firm conviction that education is something done by those in the know to those who are ignorant' and that 'The attitude change required is a move away from an attitude of "power over" to one based on person-centred values' (1990: 364, 367).

Moll (1995) provides some interesting ethnographic data from his observations of a poor rural primary school in north-eastern Transvaal, which is illustrative of the predominantly authoritarian nature of education in South Africa. Moll argues that a particular perception of teaching and learning was implicated in the prevailing pedagogy. He quotes two teachers in this regard:

When these little ones speak, they must say words that I have told them to say. Otherwise what is the point of having a lesson? If I am teaching numbers, they must speak of numbers; if I am teaching letters, they must speak of letters. If they speak the things they want to, they can learn nothing.

The syllabus tells me what my students must know. My duty as a teacher is to tell them that. I do not know how they can know these things if I do not tell them.

The only time students actually spoke during a lesson was in unison with other students in the class as they repeated something either written on the blackboard or having just been said by the teacher. For over 80 per cent of the time the teacher would write on the blackboard, pausing occasionally to ask the students to repeat or copy down something. Corporal punishment was the norm with children who were noisy being called to the front and whipped across the hands using a switch from a tree. According to the teachers this happened all the time as was regarded by them as integral part of the role of 'school teacher'. The headteacher was also very authoritarian. She told the other teachers what to teach, when and how to do so and spent most of her day wandering from class to class, now and then issuing curt instructions to teachers or students.

The other side of the authoritarian coin are the expensive private schools which put the 'authority in authoritarian' through providing an education which emphasises leadership. An example is Michaelhouse School in KwaZulu Natal, which charges 32,000 rand a year and which is based on the model of the British public school. Michaelhouse operates what it calls the 'cack' system – cacks being the term by which all first years are known, meaning 'scum of the earth'. Like the 'fagging' system in British public schools, junior students are expected to serve and do tasks for senior students. In the past this was enforced with a great deal of physical punishment. Although it does not now involve this element of brutality the practice remains in place (Bauer, 1995). The essence of this practice is that the younger students serve an apprenticeship in authority commencing at the bottom of the ladder. The principle which underlies this is subordination as a necessary prerequisite for superordination, i.e. those who expect to give commands (both inside the school and later outside) should have experience of receiving them. Such future expectations of leadership are reinforced by the acknowledged elite status of the school which is manifested in its buildings and traditions and reflected in the post-school professional connections and opportunities it provides.

The Beginnings of an Alternative Education

Between the Soweto uprisings of 1976 and 1985 schools in South Africa faced serious and continual disruption in the light of a series of demonstrations, strikes and boycotts against apartheid. The popular slogan of the time was 'liberation first, education later'. Moreover, emphasis was put on comparing the poor resourcing of black education with the affluence of white education: 'White education was not, itself, subjected to a critique. Thus, for example, its undemocratic education, its individualistic orientation, its internal inequalities, were never questioned' (Wolpe, 1995: 23). In 1985, however, the emphasis of the struggle against apartheid within education began to change from an outright rejection of Bantu education to an attempt to change schools from within. The phrase that was used to describe the new approach to education was 'people's education'. While this was a rejection of racism in education, Christie (1991: ch. 9) describes how it was expressed in very general terms and made much use of traditional socialist language such as serving the interests of the masses and creating a working-class consciousness. However, one more specific theme that emerged from the discussion surrounding people's education was the need to educate for participation. At one of the Education Crisis Conferences at the time, for example, it was described as an education which:

> prepares people for total human liberation; one which helps people to be creative, to develop a critical mind. to help people to analyse; one that prepares people for full participation in all social, political or cultural spheres of society. (Mkatshwa quoted in Christie, 1991: 271)

One influence on ANC educational thinking was the school established on a sisal estate called Mazimbu near Morogoro in Tanzania in 1978 to cope with the increasing number of exiled young people leaving South Africa after the Soweto uprisings of 1976. It became known formally as the Solomon Mahlangu Freedom College (SOMAFCO) after a combatant of the ANC's armed wing, Umkhonto we Sizwe, who was executed in South Africa in 1979. Like the EPLF Zero School in Eritrea and the SWAPO school in Loudima, SOMAFCO was inevitably something of 'a window to a future South Africa' (Serote, 1992: 49). One student at SOMAFCO interviewed about the school for a video noted that, 'We want to create what will be beneficial for our society in the future. For example, participating in the (school) administration is not something we enjoy in South Africa.' One teacher at the school that 'SOMAFCO should represent a prototype school as envisaged in the Freedom Charter and in the ANC education policy'. Mohammed Tikly, Director of the SOMAFCO Campus between 1983 and 1987, put it that 'We are trying to create here, in simple terms, a new person, a new type of South African, who will be dedicated to democratic values, who will be non-racist in his or her perception of society and also be committed to social justice' (ANC, 1989: 15).

Not surprisingly political education played a major role in the school's curriculum from nursery school to senior secondary school, particularly in terms of the ANC's perspective on the anti-apartheid struggle. At this stage in the middle of an armed conflict, with a clear oppressor in the Freirean sense and with liberal use of revolutionary language, it is also not surprising that the political education as described in detail by one teacher in the school (Pampallis, 1988) now reads like an inconsistent mixture of political indoctrination and political education for democracy. What is undoubtedly of more lasting significance was the attempt to establish a school organisational and learning climate that was significantly less authoritarian and more democratic than the model prevalent under Bantu education. One form four secondary student, for example, noted that:

> I never imagined that there could be progress without corporal pun-
> ishment or that persuasion could be used as a corrective measure.
> Under Bantu education everything comes from above but here the
> situation is different because we are given the chance to think for
> ourselves . . . Being able to work through a student council one could
> choose many avenues of expression or activities. I am now head of the
> news committee which daily monitors, writes up and delivers news
> to the students and the community. Bantu education teachers came
> to the classroom merely to do their duty. Whether the student grasps
> the subject matter or not is of no concern to them. At SOMAFCO the
> teachers are concerned about the individual progress of the students.
> (ANC, 1985: 11)

Another commented that:

> Here I feel free to say whatever I want to. At home we had prefects
> and class monitors. It was as if they were trading with the teachers
> and reporting us. They represented the teachers to us more than us to
> the teachers. At home we were fighting for a students' representative
> council at our school, but when I came here I found that it was normal.
> (ANC, 1989: 15)

As these two quotations suggest, and in tune with the demands of
students in South Africa during the boycotts, the secondary school
provided opportunities for students to learn to operate democratically
and to administer their own affairs. The Students' Council was headed
by a six-member Executive Committee, five of whose members were
elected directly by the whole student body and one of whom (the
political commissar) was appointed by the school authorities. The
remainder of the Student Council consisted of the chairpersons of
the sixteen committees covering such functions as Culture, Sports,
Entertainment, Labour, Hostels, Catering, Disciplinary etc.

However, as one former teacher at SOMAFCO has noted, consistent
implementation of more democratic teaching and learning relationships was hampered by the fact that:

> most of the South Africans who came together together to establish and
> run it were newly arrived exiles who had had no other experience except
> with education under domination in Bantu education. There has not been
> any training for the new proactive situation and skills demanded by
> the enormity and challenge of the task were scarce. This demonstrated
> itself in the difficulty in the interpretation and application of the ANC
> education policy and the lack of skills to translate political ideas and
> ideals into practice. (Serote, 1992: 56)

One overseas volunteer who worked at SOMAFCO between 1982
and 1986 produced a study which compared the student-centred
ideals of ANC educational policy with the realities at SOMAFCO

as she observed them. She concludes that the authoritarian and rote learning emphasis of existing South African education was difficult to overcome rapidly as it was so built into both students' and staff expectations of what schools and classrooms looked like. For example, although students certainly played an active and participant role in the school and staff student relationships were more friendly and caring than in conventional schools:

> In class, nevertheless, there often still was a very considerable gap between teachers and students. Some students tended to just keep the attitudes they had in South Africa towards their teachers (whose main ingredients seemed to be fear and a feeling of antagonism), and for other students it took time to realise that the teacher–student relationship could be different. A number of teachers had the same problem; they relied to a large extent on an outward show of authority. There was also quite some insistence from the side of the leadership on symbols of respect for teachers in the classroom (e.g. students were expected to stand up when the teacher entered). I have the impression that there was great fear and that a more equal relationship would easily lead to a sort of loss of the teachers' authority in class. And it is very well possible that this fear was more or less justified, in the sense that a change always needs time. I think this problem was caused by a number of reasons: lack of pedagogical and didactical training; and/or having had no experience of different ways of dealing with students; and/or teachers having not enough knowledge of their subject to feel secure enough to be challenged. (Jacobse, 1988: 46–7)

Such a note of caution about the problematic, slow and long-term nature of fundamental educational change in teaching–learning relationships in one school should be a salient reminder of the difficulty of overhauling an entire educational system. Since 1994 the ANC-led government has embarked on that very process.

Education Policy since 1994

The release of Nelson Mandela and the unbanning of the ANC in 1990, and the political negotiations with the Nationalist Party that ensued, took place immediately after a momentous period of world history. In 1989 the communist regimes of eastern Europe had finally collapsed – meaning not only that it was difficult for South Africa to claim that it was the last bulwark against communism but also that the ANC rapidly moved from a language of socialism to a language of democracy, pluralism and human rights. Following the election of 1994 this was also rapidly reflected in education policy.

In March 1995 the new government produced its first major white paper on education and training. This is an important document as it encapsulates the new democratic philosophy of education in South Africa. It is therefore worth quoting at some length:

> The realisation of democracy, liberty, equality, justice and peace are necessary conditions for the full pursuit and enjoyment of lifelong learning. It should be a goal of education and training policy to enable a democratic, free, equal, just and peaceful society to take root and prosper in our land, on the basis that all South Africans without exception share the same inalienable rights, equal citizenship, and common national destiny, and that all forms of bias (especially racial, ethnic and gender) are dehumanising. This requires the active encouragement of mutual respect for our people's diverse religious, cultural and language traditions, their right to enjoy and practice these in peace and without hindrance, and the recognition that these are a source of strength for their own communities and the unity of the nation . . . The education system must counter the legacy of violence by promoting the values underlying democratic processes and the charter of fundamental rights, the importance of due process of law and exercise of civic responsibility, and by teaching values and skills for conflict management and conflict resolution, the importance of mediation, and the benefits of toleration and cooperation . . . The curriculum, teaching methods and textbooks at all levels and in all programmes of education and training, should encourage independent and critical thought, the capacity to question, enquire, reason, weigh evidence and form judgements, achieve understanding, recognise the provisional nature of most human knowledge and communicate clearly. (Department of Education, 1995a: 22)

In 1996 the government published a white paper on the organisation and funding of schools which translates this democratic philosophy into what it terms 'democratic institutional management': 'A school governance structure should involve all stakeholder groups,in active and responsible roles, encourage tolerance, rational discussion and collective decision-making' (Department of Education, 1996: 16). The legislation stemming from this document will make it illegal not to manage schools democratically. All schools will have student representative councils and in secondary schools students – along with parents, teachers, non-teaching staff, the principal and members of the community – will be elected on to the school governing body which will be a powerful body controlling broad policy, staffing, admissions, curriculum, finance, maintenance, communication and community services.

There is also considerable awareness of the enormous implications of this significant move from authoritarian to democratic school management for all those in education. The Minister of Education has established a Task Team on Educational Management Development which will report at the end of 1996 in order to begin to address the issue which it encapsulates as follows:

> With a revolution in education management going on, there has been
> little substantial planning so far about how best to set in place the
> structures, systems, processes and procedures appropriate to South
> Africa's new management style in education. Training for leaders
> and managers – whether they are in schools, governing bodies, or
> in administrations – continues to be ad hoc and rather hit and miss,
> and the numbers who are reached are small in relation to the need.
> (Centre for Education Policy Development, 1996: 1)

The curriculum framework discussion document produced by the
government at the end of 1995 also clearly signals a move away from
a prescriptive, rigid and centralised curriculum to a more flexible,
negotiated, decentralised curriculum based on outcomes rather than
detailed content. The curriculum framework aims at helping to foster
a democratic society and among the principles informing the design
of a new curriculum are:

- Learner-centredness – that the curriculum should put learners
  rather than subject content first by recognising and building on
  their knowledge, skills, abilities and experience and responding
  to their needs. The development of learners' ability to work
  co-operatively and independently will also be encouraged.
- Relevance – including the necessary competences and skills
  required for active social, political and economic life.
- Nation-building and non-discrimination – including mutual
  respect for diverse cultural and value systems, co-operation, civic
  responsibility and the ability to participate in all aspects of society and the protection and advancement of basic human rights
  irrespective of gender, race, class, creed, geographic location or
  age.
- Critical and creative thinking – including an acknowledgement of
  the provisional, contested and changing nature of knowledge, the
  need to balance independent, individualised thinking with social
  responsibility and the ability to function as part of a group,
  community or society and the need to change the perception of
  teachers as dispensers of knowledge so that learners are valued
  as equal and active participants in learning and development
  processes. (Department of Education 1995b)

Teacher education in South Africa in the past has contributed to,
rather than challenged, the authoritarian nature of schools. This is
because the training colleges themselves are often managed and
administered like secondary schools rather than tertiary institutions
and have uniforms, rigid timetables and, in some cases, the ringing

of bells. The curriculum is often overcrowded, especially for primary teacher training students, and this encourages reliance on whole class teaching and the memorisation and testing of 'facts'. One report on the nature of teacher training colleges in KwaZulu Natal, for example, noted that teaching was dominated by formal lectures and that lecturers failed to adopt the same teaching methods that they were advocating to students. The report also commented that students and staff played only a very limited role in college management. Staff meetings were for most of the time devoid of discussion and the notion of student democracy was non-existent. The hierarchical management structure did not facilitate independent initiatives and at most colleges there was no internal forum where ideas could be exchanged and grievances aired. Students were therefore taught about school management and organisation but did not have an opportunity to practice it at college, while the organisational style and management of colleges tended to promote passive, uncritical and introspective responses from staff (Salmon and Woods, 1991).

As was argued in chapter 7, reform of teacher education is important in helping to break the cycle of authoritarianism in schools. The content and processes of teacher education must become more congruent with a more democratic form of education. A start has been made at the policy level in South Africa with the publication of new *Norms and Standards for Teacher Education* (Committee on Teacher Education Policy, 1996). However, as the preface to this document points out, it is not merely a revision of existing criteria but a radical paradigm shift in that it embodies a move away from an approach which simply listed the subjects to be covered to one which stresses aims, competencies and outcomes. The Norms and Standards are quite explicit in their about their political stance:

> In South Africa, teacher education would have to take account of the inequities in society, the transition to a democratic, non-racial, non-sexist, equitable society and create an awareness of the freedoms and responsibilities contained and implicit in the sections on human rights in the South African constitution. (1996: 7)

This is reflected in the nature of the knowledge, skills and values that teacher education is now supposed to cultivate. The following are some examples:

Knowledge

• of rights accorded to the individual and to groups constituted in terms of freedom of association;

- of gender issues;
- of sexuality and family education;
- of parental involvement in education;
- of environmental issues, both locally and globally;
- of teachers' rights and responsibilities; and
- of the relationship between education on the one hand and community and nation-building on the other.

Skills

- the ability to use language for effective learning and thinking, for developing proficiency in interpersonal relationships and for critical reflection;
- thinking skills in the curriculum, both domain specific and generic;
- the ability to be self-reflective and aware of one's own learning strategies, thinking processes and teaching styles, and to be able to articulate them to assist students in their learning;
- the facilitation of learner-centred classroom practice and collaborative learning;
- a resource-based approach to teaching and learning;
- the ability to deal with human rights issues, including gender issues;
- the ability to reflect critically on their own practice;
- the ability to reflect critically on education in society; and
- being autonomous, flexible, creative and responsible agents for change in response to the educational challenges of the day and in relation to the espoused aims of education in South Africa.

Values

- respect for the individual;
- sensitivity to gender issues;
- education for critical, responsible and useful citizenship in order to equip the individual for service in the wider community and environment;
- values as encompassed in the human rights manifesto;
- a recognition and understanding of the approaches to multi-culturalism; and
- community involvement, promoting adaptability and tolerance in a multi-cultural society.

The document also provides a definition of what it sees as the perfect teacher in the new South Africa:

In brief, teacher education should develop teachers with a sense of vision which reflects values aimed at enabling pupils to develop as persons who are well-informed, rational, reflective, critical choosers and yet are tolerant and compassionate human beings who have the courage to take risks, the fortitude to handle failure and a belief in the value of life. These values can only be developed in an institution of which the ethos demonstrates such values in operation. (1996: 12)

It is perhaps not surprising that next to this paragraph in the author's copy of the document somebody has scribbled 'angels and saints'! However, while the document may be aiming rather high in the short term, education in the past has often not been sufficiently clear about its goals and the processes and structures required to achieve them, and it is therefore important that a sense of purpose and direction is provided by making these clear and explicit. The document is also honest and realistic about the difficulties that will be faced in working towards this ideal type of teacher education and the time it will take to accomplish:

The aims and competencies listed below are likely to make exceedingly heavy demands both on teachers and teacher educators. They reflect the ideal towards which teacher education should be directed, but they should be implemented judiciously, allowing time for reflection. The inclusion of aims, competencies and course content will have to be prioritised by the teacher educators offering the various programmes. (1996: 6)

A Case Study School

There are many obstacles to successful post-apartheid educational reform in South Africa and these are discussed more fully in Harber (1997). However, the purpose of the next two sections of this chapter is to explore positive examples of what is possible in terms of education for democracy in the new South Africa.

A recent study of racial desegregation in fifteen secondary and eleven primary schools in KwaZulu Natal found that although the students were now mixed in the schools, there was a general attitude of 'business as usual'. Despite the change in student population many of the schools were essentially the same as before and little attention had been paid to school organisation or staff and student development (Naidoo, 1996). However, not all schools have remained the same. Grosvenor Girls High School in Durban, for example, provides an interesting example of the sort of issues faced in a school that has both desegregated and begun to democratise its organisational structures in order to make them more suitable for the new context.The following account is based on school documents and on interviews and observation carried out at the school during 1996.

Until 1991 the school, which is an all-girls school, was all-white by law but by 1996 the school's student population had become sixty per cent white and forty per cent black. In many ways the ethos of the school remains quite traditional through its uniform, ceremonies and activities. However, while there has been continuity there has also been change. The headteacher has very clear views on the type of school that is required in the context of the new South Africa which are, for example, expressed in the annual school magazine. In 1994 she talks of the 'rich diversity of human experiences and cultures and the common problems we share as a school community . . . as part of the South African community' and she notes that 'The inculcation of a democratic culture and the development of a strong family spirit in our school has been instrumental in helping the girls build bridges of tolerance, acceptance and unity among themselves'. In 1995 the case for a more democratic school is put as follows:

> The most significant set of new challenges which has accompanied our growth is our development as a large multicultural school for girls in a new democratic South Africa. Having girls of different culture, religion, race, language and skin colour in a school does not necessarily make it multicultural. A school which is truly multi-cultural is one in which each pupil is valued equally by other pupils and by staff alike; one in which all pupils display mutual respect and make every effort to understand each person's language and culture; to respect their choice of religion; their right to voice their opinions and to accept each person's individuality. A truly multicultural school is one in which the pupils and staff are free from any form of discrimination or prejudice.

She also notes the need to address these issues honestly and that it will take time, but that 'the way ahead is clear – input from staff, parents and the girls at all levels of management is essential to our development'.

The direct link between democratic school structures and the now multiracial nature of the school was made at the first school assembly attended by the writer at which the head reflected directly on an altercation that had occurred the day before on the sports field about different traditions and which had degenerated into racial name-calling. The message from the head was direct and clear: anything can be debated and changed but there must be mutual respect, no aggression and the right channels must be used.

These channels are through the student representative council (SRC).

The aims of the council are fourfold:

1   To improve communication in the school.
2   To involve pupils in democratic decision making.
3   To develop leadership and responsibility.
4   To maintain the family ethos of the school.

Each of the twenty-four classes at the school elects a representative to the council from a slate of eight to ten candidates in each class. All clubs, sports, societies and pupil service groups are also represented (sixteen in all) and there eighteen prefects elected by the whole school who take responsibility for certain portfolios or areas of school life. At meetings of the SRC, at which no member of the school staff is present, class representatives raise and discuss matters brought up by their classes. As there are fifty-eight members of the SRC in all it was decided that from 1996 an executive council of seven members (a member from each year plus the head girl and deputy head girl) would be constituted which investigates issues raised by the SRC and makes decisions on the issues after debate, investigation and consultation with the school governing body. The head girl and deputy head girl chair both the executive council and the student representative council and are members of the school's governing body along with parents, teachers and members of the community. The head and deputy headgirl are indirectly elected from among the elected group of prefects after all prefects spend an orientation weekend away with each other.

One key theme of this book is that democratic skills and values are learned and that it cannot just be assumed that people will somehow develop them naturally or by chance. A lot of this learning will come from continual experience of democratic structures in schools, but in order for such structures to function as efficiently as possible as quickly as possible some built in prior training is of considerable value. At this school all class representatives undergo a training session which includes a clear description of their role and focuses on such skills as communicating effectively, handling conflict, managing a group and applying a democratic style of leadership in the classroom. An important message of this session and one which helps to differentiate a democratic education from an authoritarian one, was the realisation that mistakes would be made and that learning from mistakes is a key aspect of learning overall.

Sessions of the SRC and the executive have so far debated and influenced decisions over a whole range of issues including the nature of uniforms, the provision of a pay phone, congestion on stairways, the provision of school buses, the need for more benches around the school, the state of school toilets, the timing of assemblies and athletics meetings, the provision of school discos and student ID cards. Discussions witnessed by the writer have been enthusiastic and sometimes impassioned though always polite and friendly but have exhibited many of the classic features of democratic politics – putting a case, negotiation, give and take and decision making based on compromise.

The school has also recently embarked upon a democratic process of drafting a new key document which will embody a statement of shared values and behaviours, a new code of conduct and school rules, and a new set of disciplinary procedures in order to 'truly democratise the school thereby strengthening her position as an effective, developing multicultural school in the new South Africa'. Staff, students and parents were divided into twenty-eight workshops in which the new context for South African education was discussed along with the need for a new, agreed set of basic values and rules to fully reflect the new context. Part of this process involves the establishment of a temporary 'change committee' made up of representatives from the workshops to ensure that this process is seen through, though the SRC, school management and governing body will serve as permanent structures through which change will be managed in the long term.

How have staff and students responded to these changes? Group interviews were held with eight members of the SRC executive, eight class representatives, eight other students who held no official position, four teachers who were heads of department and four teachers without a post of responsibility. The headteacher was also formally interviewed early on in the academic year but regular informal discussion of the progress of democratisation took place during visits to the school. While the student groups had a mixed racial composition all the teachers were white. The two key findings from these interviews was that all the students and the teachers were adamant that compared with 1994 and 1995 there had been a dramatic decrease in racism and that there was now very little physical or verbal violence. Both students and teachers were clear that this could largely be attributed to the new structures and the culture of mutual respect it had helped to engender. They suggested that the decrease in tension and frustration was due to improved communication, dialogue and involvement and that the students now had a sense of control over their own lives. The openness that had resulted from the changes had enhanced awareness of, and sensitivity to, racial issues and had allowed racism to be confronted and challenged head on. Despite the time and effort required there was general agreement that a more democratic form of organisation was preferable to an authoritarian one and this view was particularly strongly expressed by students and teachers who had been at other schools.

Non-governmental Organisations

In chapter 1 it was argued that a strong civil society composed of active and democratically managed organisations was important for the future of democracy in Africa and that part of their role lay in helping to educate for democracy. South Africa has a strong tradition of non-governmental organisations, many coming into existence as a way of operating outside of the apartheid state. Some of these NGOs play an important and direct role in educating for democracy in schools where the traditional authoritarianism described earlier in this chapter provides considerable barriers to the implementation of the government's new policy framework for education. Dovey (1996), for example, provides a very useful overview of the range of South African organisations involved in education for democracy and peace. The remainder of this chapter will briefly describe the work of one such organisation in order both to highlight the type of educational work that needs to be done in assisting schools and the problems to be faced in making schools more democratic. The NGO, with which the writer has worked, operates in KwaZulu Natal (KZN), a province that has been particularly marked by violent political conflict.

The Independent Projects Trust was founded in 1990 and maintains its non-aligned status by receiving funding from private industry and charitable trusts. The IPT runs community conflict resolution workshops among, for example, traditional Zulu leaders, local government councillors, women's groups, taxi owners and residents of informal settlements (shanty towns). Since 1994, in the light of the tensions produced by the rapid desegregation of schools, they have also been working with teachers, parents and students. They have developed what they term the Schools Mediation and Reconciliation and Training Programme (SMART), which is designed to create a step-by-step process of working with schools and other education bodies to assist them to teach and use effective dispute and conflict management skills and democratic processes. SMART originally aimed to focus on teachers and students in eight schools in KZN in order to facilitate the transfer of skills in human rights, democracy and conflict resolution. The following account is based primarily on an independent evaluation carried out after one year of its operation (Foulis and Anderson, 1995).

In practice the focus has been on training teachers and lecturers in teacher training colleges rather than students as it was felt that this was a better way of maximising impact and utilising the limited resources available. A manual has been developed as the basis for training which covers the nature of conflict, communication, assertiveness, group problem solving, negotiation and mediation. Also, the types of conflict that teachers have felt that they needed to address have gone beyond racial integration to abuse within students' families, violence within the broader community, conflict between staff, conflict between governing bodies and school administration/staff, ethnic conflict and teachers dating students and subsequent discipline problems. In some schools (particularly historically African schools) the SMART workers have faced problems of low morale and lack of enthusiasm which is related to large classes, a lack of resources and an already heavy workload. However, the training has been particularly successful in schools which have committed guidance teachers who are able to be champions of the programme and where the school principal is a strong advocate of the programme. Overall, the authors of the evaluation comment positively on the role that such an organisation can play in fostering more democratic approaches to conflict management:

> In speaking to the various target groups, the evaluators have been overwhelmed at the positive response to the SMART programme. Without exception, people have acknowledged the importance of conflict resolution skills in the society in which we live, work and study. From the resolution of quarrels between peers to the mediation of differences between politicians, conflict is a part of our everyday lives. The consequences of not being able to resolve these differences are serious. The SMART programme has been operating for less than a year and has made enormous progress during this year . . . It is apparent from the comments from teachers and pupils in different schools that the SMART programme has contributed to a greater team spirit and a more conducive learning environment. The experience is also backed up by experience in American schools where truancy and suspension has declined and a more peaceful and conducive learning environment has emerged.

They add that at one secondary school 'it appears that the IPT training is reinforcing the school's new approach to discipline where they have shifted away from corporal punishment to peer mediation, largely on their own initiative' (Foulis and Anderson, 1995: 13, 10, 7).

Indeed, the evaluation suggests that one way that more teachers can be drawn into the process is if teachers in one school are informed of the success in other schools where more peaceful classroom environments have been created, suspensions and detentions have declined and distracting student behaviour reduced: 'The more more demanding environment that teachers face with bigger classes, new curricula and racial integration means that teachers are going to have to look to new ways of managing the classroom' (12).

Conclusion

From the beginnings of apartheid in 1948 until its demise in 1994 a major function of schools in South Africa was to close minds and create racial barriers. This has left a major and negative legacy of segregation, authoritarianism and violent disruption in education which reflected the wider political context of that period. The new educational policy that followed the election of an ANC-led government has begun to address these issues and there is now a clearly stated commitment to education for democracy. The achievement of more democratic schools in South Africa as elsewhere will require time, patience, good will and a great deal of effort and persistence by all concerned. However, the enhanced educational and organisational effectiveness of schools that will emerge from such a change should encourage such persistence which should in itself benefit from the pivotal role that education must play in helping to shape a democratic civic culture in South Africa in the future.

Bibliography

Abbott, I. and Mercer, D. (1989a) 'Democratic learning in teacher education: a comparative study' *Educational Review* 41(1).

Abbott, I. and Mercer, D. (1989b) 'Democratic learning: implications for teacher education' in C. Harber and R. Meighan (eds) *The Democratic School* (Ticknall: Education Now).

Admasu, G. and Alemayehu, G. (1994) *Five Years of Geography and History Ethiopian School Leaving Examinations* (Ethiopia: EMPDA).

Akintola, J. M. (1980) *Introduction to Nigerian Educational Research Council Social Studies: Teaching Issues and Problems* (Benin: Ethiope Publishing Corporation).

Al-Salmi, T. (1994) *Teacher Education in Oman*. Unpublished Ph.D. thesis, University of Birmingham.

Alaro, A. (1985) The Main Trends, Needs and Priorities in Social Studies Education in Ethiopia.

Allen-Mills, T. (1987) 'Banda makes Latin a must at Africa's Eton', *The Independent*, 8 December 1987.

Allport, G. (1958) *The Nature of Prejudice* (Cambridge, Mass.: Addison Wesley).

Almedon, A. (1994) *Political Learning in Eritrea*. Unpublished Certificate of Education Essay, University of Birmingham.

Almond, G. (1970) *Political Development: Essays in Heuristic Theory* (Boston: Little Brown).

Almond, G. (1993) 'The Return to Political Culture', in L. Diamond (ed.) *Political Culture and Democracy in Developing Countries* (Boulder: Lynne Rienner).

Almond, G. and Powell, B. (1966) *Comparative Politics: A Developmental Approach* (Boston: Little Brown).

Almond, G. and Verba, S. (1963) *The Civic Culture* (Princeton: Princeton University Press).

Alverson, H. (1978) *Mind in the Heart of Darkness* (New Haven: Yale University Press).

Amukugo, E. (1993) *Education and Politics in Namibia* (Windhoek: New Namibia Books).

ANC (1985) *SOMAFCO Official Opening 21–23 August 1985* (ANC Dept. of Publicity and Information).

ANC (1989) *Education for Liberation: The Solomon Mahlangu Freedom College, 10 Years 1979–1989* (Lusaka: ANC Department of Education).

Andersson, I., Callewaert, S. and Kallos, D. (1991) *Teacher Education Reform for Namibia* (Windhoek: Report Submitted to the Ministry of Education, Culture, Youth and Sport).

Angula, N. (1982) 'The relationship between education and society: Namibia in the conditions of the national liberation struggle after independence'. Paper presented to SWAPO seminar on *Education and Culture for Liberation*, Lusaka.

Apter, D. (1957) *Ghana in Transition* (Princeton: Princeton University Press).

Apter, D. (1965) *The Politics of Modernisation* (Chicago: Chicago University Press).

Aristotle (1962) *The Politics* (Harmondsworth: Penguin).

ASSP (1979) Report on the Seminar of Peace Education,·International Understanding and Respect for Human Rights, Nairobi.

ASSP (1985) Report of the Seminar of the Co-ordinating Committee, Nairobi.

Avalos, B. (1991) *Approaches to Teacher Education: Initial Teacher Education* (London: Commonwealth Secretariat).

Baliloko, C. M. and Malie, E. M. (1979) Paper on Lesotho at the Regional Workshop on Environmental Education in the School Curriculum held in Lusaka, Zambia.

Ball, S. (1987) *The Micro-Politics of the School* (London: Methuen).

Barth, J. (1986) African Social Studies Programme as Leadership Education Toward Nation Building. *African Social Studies Forum* 1(1).

Bartholemew, J. (1978) 'Schooling teachers: the myth of the liberal college', in G. Whitty and M. Young (eds) *Explorations in the Politics of School Knowledge* (Driffield: Nafferton).

Bauer, C. (1996) 'The lofty redbrick tradition', *Sunday Times*, 23 June.

Bayart, J-F. (1993) *The State in Africa: The Politics of the Belly* (London: Longman).

Bethell, G. (1990) *Evaluation of Examination Needs of Primary and Secondary Schools* (Windhoek: University of Cambridge Local Examinations Syndicate for the Ministry of Education and Culture).

Binder, L. et al. (1971) *Crises and Sequences in Political Development* (Princeton: Princeton University Press).

Bratton, M. (1994) 'International versus domestic pressures for democratisation in Africa'. Paper presented at a conference on The End of the Cold War: Effects and Prospects for Asia and Africa (London: School of Oriental and African Studies).

British Council (1993) *Development Priorities: Guidelines on Good Government* (Manchester: The British Council).

Brock-Utne, B., Appiah-Endresen, I. and Oliver, C. (1994) *Evaluation of the NAMAS Support to Mweshipandeka Senior Secondary School* (Windhoek: Namibia Association of Norway).

Brown, S. (1985) 'Diplomacy by other means – SWAPO's liberation war', in C. Leys and J. Saul *Namibia's Liberation Struggle* (London: James Currey).

Brown, S. T. (1985) Main Trends, Needs and Priorities in Social Studies Education and Training in Liberia. ASSP Report of the Seminar of the Co-ordinating Committee. Nairobi.

Canadian International Development Agency (1993) *Rights, Democratisation, Governance and Development: An Issues Paper for CIDA's Policy Committee* (Quebec: CIDA).

Carnoy, M. and Samoff, J. (1990) *Education and Social Transition in the Third World* (Princeton: Princeton University Press).

Centre for Education Policy Development (1996) *Task Team on Education Management Development* (Braamfontein).

Centre for the Advancement of Science and Maths Education (1995) *A Profile* (Durban: University of Natal).

Chamba, S. R. (1974/5) Civics Teaching in Zambian Secondary Schools. *Zambian Educational Journal* 1(4).

Chase, N. (1987) 'Education in Katatura', in C. Von Garnier (ed.) *Katatura Revisited* (Windhoek: Roman Catholic Church).

Chazan, N. (1988) 'Ghana: Problems of governance and the emergence of civil society', in L. Diamond, J. Linz and S. Lipset (eds) *Democracy in Developing Countries: Africa* (London: Adamantine Press).

Chazan, N. (1993) 'Between liberalism and statism: African political cultures and democracy', in L. Diamond (ed.) *Political Culture and Democracy in Developing Countries* (Boulder: Lynne Rienner).

Christie, P. (1991) *The Right to Learn* (Johannesburg: SACHED/Ravan).

Cleaver, T. and Wallace, M. (1990) *Namibia: Women at War* (London: Zed Books).

Coleman, J. (1958) *Nigeria: Background to Nationalism* (Berkeley: University of California Press).

Coleman, J. (ed.) (1965) *Education and Political Development* (Princeton: University of Princeton Press).

Committee on Teacher Education Policy (1996) *Norms and Standards for Teacher Education* (Pretoria).

Connell, D. (1993) *Against All Odds* (Trenton, NJ: The Red Sea Press).

Connolly, R. (1980) Freire, Praxis and Education. In *Literacy and Revolution: the Pedagogy of Paulo Freire*, ed. R. Mackie (London: Pluto Press).

Conway, M. and Damico, S. (1993) 'Facing up to Multiculturalism Means as Ends in Democratic Education'. Paper Delivered to the International Conference on Education for Democracy in a Multicultural Society, Jerusalem, Israel.

Cook, S. (1969) 'Motives in conceptual analysis of attitude-related behaviour', in W. J. Arnold and I. Levine (eds) *Nebraska Symposium on Motivation*, vol. 18 (Lincoln, Nebraska: University of Nebraska Press).

Cooksey, B. (1986) 'Policy and practice in Tanzanian secondary education since 1967', *International Journal of Educational Development* 6(3): 183–202.

Dadey, A. (1990) *The Role of the Headmaster in the Administration of Secondary Schools in Ghana*. Unpublished Ph.D. thesis, University of Birmingham.

Dahlstrom, L. et al. (1989) *The Integrated Teacher Training Programme 1986–1989* (Umea: Pedagogiska Institutionen/ITTP).

DANIDA (1993) *Human Rights and Democracy* (Copenhagen: Ministry of Foreign Affairs).

Datta, A. (1984) *Education and Society: A Sociology of African Education* (London: Macmillan).

Davidson, B. (1980) 'An historical note', in B. Davidson, L. Cliffe and B. Selassie (eds) *Behind the War in Eritrea* (Nottingham: Spokesman).

Davidson, B., Cliffe, L. and Selassie, B. (eds) (1980) *Behind the War in Eritrea* (Nottingham: Spokesman).

Davies, L. (1993) 'Teachers as implementers or resisters', *International Journal of Educational Development* 13(2).

Department of Education (1995a) *White Paper on Education and Training* (Pretoria).

Department of Education (1995b) *Curriculum Framework for General and Further Education and Training* (Pretoria).

Department of Education (1996) *The Organisation, Governance and Funding of Schools* (Pretoria).

Diamond, L. (1988a) 'Introduction: Roots of failure, seeds of hope', in L. Diamond, J. Linz and S. Lipset (eds) *Democracy in Developing Countries: Africa* (London: Adamantine Press).

Diamond, L. (1988b) 'Nigeria: pluralism, statism and the struggle for democracy', in L. Diamond, J. Linz and S. Lipset (eds) *Democracy in Developing Countries: Africa* (London: Adamantine Press).

Diamond, L. (ed.) (1993) *Political Culture and Democracy in Developing Countries* (Boulder: Lynne Rienner).

Diamond, L. (1994) 'Civil society and democratic consolidation: building a culture of democracy in a new South Africa', in H. Giliomee, L. Schlemmer and S. Hauptfleisch (eds) *The Bold Experiment: South Africa's New Democracy* (Cape Town: Southern Book Publishers).

Dimmock, C. (1995) 'Building democracy in a school setting: the principal's role', in J. Chapman, D. Aspin (eds) *Creating and Managing the Democratic School* (London: The Falmer Press).

Dines, M. (1980) 'The land, the people and the revolution', in B. Davidson, L. Cliffe and B. Selassis (eds) *Behind the War in Eritrea* (Nottingham: Spokesman).

Dobell, L. (1995) 'SWAPO in Office', in C. Leys and J. Saul *Namibia's Liberation Struggle* (London: James Currey).

Dove, L. (1986) *Teachers and Teacher Education in Developing Countries* (Beckenham: Croom Helm).

Dovey, V. (1996) 'Exploring peace education in South African settings', *Peabody Journal of Education* 71(3).

Dubey, D. et al. (1979) *The Sociology of Nigerian Education* (London: Macmillan).

Dubey, D. L. (1980) Problems and Issues in Teaching the Methods of Social Studies.

In *Nigerian Educational Research Council Social Studies: Teaching Issues and problems*. Ethiope Publishing Corporation, Benin.

Duodu, C. (1992) 'Generals who steal our freedoms', *The Observer*, 27 June 1993.

Ehman, L. (1980) 'The American High School in the Political Socialisation Process', *Review of Educational Research* 50.

Eleazu, U. (1977) *Federalism and Nation Building* (Devon: Stockwell).

Elietinize, F. M. S. (1981) *Problems of Teaching Political Education in Secondary Schools*. MA dissertation, University of Dar es Salaam.

Ellis, J. (1984) *Education, Repression and Liberation* (London: Catholic Institute for International Relations).

Enslin, K. (1984) 'The role of fundamental pedagogics in the formulation of educational policy in South Africa', in P. Kallaway (ed.) *Apartheid and Education* (Johannesburg: Ravan Press).

EPLF (1982) *Eritrean National Curriculum*.

Fagerlind, I. and Saha, L. (1989) *Education and National Development* (Oxford: Pergamon).

FINNIDA (1991) *Development Co-operation and Processes Towards Democracy* (Helsinki: Ministry for Foreign Affairs).

Firebrace, J. and Holland, S. (1985) *Never Kneel Down: Drought, Development and Liberation in Eritrea* (Trenton, NJ: Red Sea Press).

Foulis, C-A. and Anderson, D. (1995) *Evaluation of the SMART Programme within the IPT* (Durban: Olive).

Freire, P. (1972) *Pedagogy of the Oppressed* (London: Sheed and Ward).

Freire, P. (1975) *The Politics of Education* (London: Macmillan).

Freire, P. (1978) *Pedagogy in Process: The Letters to Guinea-Bissau* (London: Writers and Readers Publishing Co-operative).

Frykholm, C-U. (1995) *National Evaluation of the Basic Education Teacher Diploma Broad Curriculum Issues* (Okahandja: National Institute for Education Development).

Fuller, B. (1991) *Growing Up Modern* (London: Routledge).

Gatter, F. et al. (1987) *100 Years of Colonialism, Neocolonialism and Struggle for Freedom: Education for Liberation* (Bremen: University of Bremen African Archive).

Ginsberg, M. (1988) *Contradictions in Teacher Education and Society* (Lewes: The Falmer Press).

Gitonga, A. (1988) 'The meaning and foundations of democracy', in W. Oyugi, E. Atieno Odhiambo, M. Chege and A. Gitonga (eds) *Democratic Theory and Practice in Africa* (London: James Currey).

Gordon, T. (1986) *Democracy in One School* (Lewes: The Falmer Press).

Government of Eritrea (1993) *Birth of a Nation* (Asmara: Department of External Affairs).

Greenland, J. (1983) *In-service Training of Primary Teachers in Africa* (Basingstoke: Macmillan).

Gustaffson, I. (1987) 'Work as education – perspectives on the role of work in current educational reform in Zimbabwe'. In *Vocationalizing Education*, edited by J. Lauglo and K. Lillis (Oxford: Pergamon Press).

Hake, J. (1972) *Child Rearing Practices in Northern Nigeria* (Ibadan: Ibadan University Press).

Handy, C. (1984) *Taken for Granted? Looking at Schools as Organisations* (York: Longmans).

Handy, C. and Aitken, R. (1986) *Understanding Schools as Organisations* (Harmondsworth: Penguin).

Harber, C. (1989) *Politics in African Education* (London: Macmillan).

Harber, C. (1991) 'International contexts for political education', *Educational Review* 43(3): 245–56.

Harber, C. (1992) *Democratic Learning and Learning Democracy* (Ticknall: Education Now).

Harber, C. (1993) 'Overseas students and democratic learning', *British Journal of In-Service Education* 19.

Harber, C. (1995) *Developing Democratic Education* (Ticknall: Education Now).

Harber, C. (1997) 'Redress and access: educational reform in the new South Africa', in L. Buchert (ed.) *Education Reform in the South in the 1990's* (Paris: UNESCO).

Harber, C. and Meighan, R. (1986) 'A case study of democratic learning in teacher education', *Educational Review* 38(3).

Harber, C. and Meighan, R. (1989) *The Democratic School* (Ticknall: Education Now).

Harber, C. and Davies, L. (1997) *The Post-Bureaucratic School: School Management and School Effectiveness in Developing Countries* (London: Cassell).

Hawes, H. (1979) *Curriculum and Reality in African Primary Schools* (Harlow: Longman).

Healey, J. and Robinson, M. (1992) *Democracy, Governance and Economic Policy: Sub-Saharan Africa in Comparative Perspective* (London: Overseas Development Institute).

Helbig, L. (1989) *Schools in Resistance* (Bremen: Centre for African Studies, University of Bremen).

Hepburn, M. (1984) 'Democratic schooling – five perspectives from research', *International Journal of Political Education* 6: 245–62.

Herbstein, D. and Evenson, J. (1989) *The Devils Are Among Us: The War for Namibia* (London: Zed Books).

Heyneman, S. (1995) 'Good educational governance: an American export', *The American School Board Journal* 16.

Higgott, R. (1983) *Political Development Theory* (London: Croom Helm).

Hinzen, H. and Hundsdorfer, V. (1979) *The Tanzanian Experience* (London: Evans).

Hiskett, M. (1975) 'Islamic education in the traditional and state systems in northern Nigeria', in G. Brown and M. Hiskett (eds) *Conflict and Harmony in Education in Tropical Africa* (London: George Allen and Unwin).

Holdstock, T. (1990) 'Violence in schools: discipline', in B. McKendrick and W. Hoffman (eds) *People and Violence in South Africa* (Oxford: Oxford University Press).

Holm, J. (1988) 'Botswana: a paternalistic democracy', in L. Diamond, J. Linz and S. Lipset (eds) *Democracy in Developing Countries: Africa* (London: Adamantine Press).

Hope, S. (1993) 'A theory for transformative action', in K. Prah (ed.) *Social Science Research Priorities for Namibia* (Windhoek: University of Namibia and the Council for the Development of Economic and Social Research in Africa).

Huband, M. (1992) 'The disintegration of Somalia', *The Guardian* 7 August 1992.

Ichilov, O. (1991) 'Political socialisation and schooling effects among Israeli adolescents', *Comparative Education Review* 35(3).

Illich, I. (1971) *Deschooling Society* (Harmondsworth: Penguin).

Inkeles, A. (1969a) 'Participant citizenship in six developing countries', *American Political Science Review* 43: 1122–33.

Inkeles, A. (1969b) 'Making men modern', *American Journal of Sociology* 75: 208–25.

Inkeles, A. and Smith, D. (1974) *Becoming Modern* (London: Heinemann).

Institute for Curriculum Development (1992) *Moral and Civic Education in the Eritrean Curriculum* (Asmara: Ministry of Education).

Institute for Curriculum Development (1993) *The role of History in Morality and Civics Education* (Asmara: Ministry of Education).

Iyob, R. (1995) *The Eritrean Struggle for Independence: Domination, Resistance, Nationalism 1941–1993* (Cambridge: Cambridge University Press).

Jackson, R. and Rosberg, C. (1982) *Personal Rule in Black Africa: Prince, Autocrat, Prophet, Tyrant* (Berkeley: University of California Press).

Jacobse, J. (1988) *Developing Education Against Apartheid for Liberation* (Holland: Wageningen Agricultural University).

Jansen, J. (1991) 'The state and curriculum in the transition to socialism: The Zimbabwean Experience', *Comparative Education* 35(1).

Jensen, K. and Walker, S. (1989) *Towards Democratic Schooling* (Milton Keynes: Open University Press).

John, P. and Osborn, A. (1992) 'The influence of school ethos on pupils' citizenship attitudes', *Educational Review* 44(2).

Kabau, I. N. (1983) *The Teaching of Social Studies: Instructional Problems Facing Teachers in the Pilot Primary Schools of Central Province Kenya.* M.Ed. dissertation, University of Nairobi.

Kajubi, W. S. (1985) The Development of Social Studies Education in Uganda, Report of the Co-ordinating Committee of ASSP, Nairobi.

Kallaway, P. (ed.) *Apartheid and Education* (Johannesburg: Ravan Press).

Katjavivi, P. (1988) *A History of Resistance in Namibia* (London: James Currey).

Kelly, A. (1986) *Knowledge and Curriculum Planning* (London: Harper and Row).

Kenya Institute of Education (1987) *Social Education and Ethics* (Nairobi).

Kinnock, G. (1988) *Eritrea: Images of War and Peace* (London: Chatto and Windus).

Kisanga, M. (1986) On the Implications of the Principle of Pupil, Parent and Community Participation in the Management of Formal and Non-Formal Educational Institutions and Activities Survey for UNESCO. Unpublished, Dar Es Salaam.

Konig, B. (1983) *Namibia: The Ravages of War* (London: International Defence and Aid Fund for Southern Africa).

Kotta, M. (1986) *Tutors and Student-Teachers' Reactions to Discovery Methods in Diploma Colleges of Education.* Unpublished MA dissertation, University of Dar Es Salaam.

Kpundeh, S. J. (1992) *Democratisation in Africa: African Views, African Voices* (Washington: National Academy Press).

La Palombara, J. (1963) *Bureaucracy and Political Development* (Princeton: University of Princeton Press).

La Palombara, J. and Weiner, M. (eds) (1966) *Political Parties and Political Development* (Princeton: Princeton University Press).

Lacville, R. (1996) 'Beacon of hope in Mali', *Guardian Weekly*, 14 April 1996.

Le Vine, R. (1966) *Dreams and Deeds: Achievement Motivation in Nigeria* (Chicago: University of Chicago Press).

Leu, C. (1980) 'Colonial education and African resistance in Namibia', in A. Mugomba and M. Nyaggah (eds) *Independence Without Freedom* (Santa Barbara: ABC-Clio).

Leys, C. (1996) *The Rise and Fall of Development Theory* (London: James Currey).

Leys, C. and Saul, J. (1995) *Namibia's Liberation Struggle* (London: James Currey).

Loum, O. S. (1985) Social Studies Education and Training in the Gambia. Report of the Seminar of the Co-ordinating Committee of ASSP, Nairobi.

Lynch, J. (1992) *Education for Citizenship in a Multicultural Society* (Cassell: London).

Maleri, L. C. (1983) Implementation of Social Studies in Lesotho. Project for Postgraduate Diploma in Curriculum Development, University of Nairobi.

Mannathoko, C. (1995) *Gender, Ideology and the State in Botswana's Teacher Education.* Unpublished Ph.D. thesis, University of Birmingham.

Mazrui, A. (1983) 'Political engineering in Africa', *International Social Science Journal* 25(2).

Mbilinyi, M. (1979) 'Secondary education' in H. Hinzen and V. H. Hunsdorfer (eds) *The Tanzanian Experience* (London: Evans).

Mbilinyi, M. et al. (1991) *Education in Tanzania with a Gender Perspective* (Dar Es Salaam: SIDA).

Mbugua, N. W. (1987) *A Study of the Problems Affecting Implementation of Geography, History and Civics (Combined Social Studies) in Selected Primary colleges in Kenya.* M.Ed. dissertation, Kenyatta University, Nairobi.

Mbuyi, D. (1988) 'Texts and National Integration in East Africa', *Prospects* 18, 4.

Mc Kay, V. and Romm, N. (1995) 'The practice of discipline in education', in V. McKay (ed.) *A Sociology of Educating* (Johannesburg: Lexicon).

Meighan, R. (1994) *The Freethinkers' Guide to the Educational Universe* (Nottingham: Educational Heretics Press).

Meighan, R. and Harber, C. (1986) 'Democratic learning in teacher education: a review of experience at one institution', *Journal of Education for Teaching* 12.

Meighan, R., Harber, C. and Meighan, J. (1989) 'Democratic practice a missing item on the agenda of teacher education', in C. Harber and R. Meighan (eds) *The Democratic School* (Ticknall: Education Now).

Merryfield, M. (1986) *Social Studies Education and National Development in Selected African*

Nations. Unpublished Ph.D. thesis, University of Indiana.

Mgulambwa, A. C., Malekala, G. A., Meekwa, V. M. and Chipindula, D. C. (1985) The Teaching of Political Education in Secondary Schools and Colleges of Education in Tanzania Mainland. Report submitted to the Department of Education, University of Ministry of Education (1979) *National Policy on School Councils* (Dar Es Salaam: Government Printer).

Ministry of Education and Culture (1991a) *Report on the Monitoring of Junior Secondary Curriculum Reform, Grade 8* (Windhoek).

Ministry of Education and Culture (1991b) *Annual Report for the Year Ending 31 December 1991* (Windhoek).

Ministry of Education and Culture (1992a) *A Report on a Course in Educational Management for Inspectors of Education* (Windhoek).

Ministry of Education and Culture (1992b) *A report on a Sensitization Seminar on Management of Basic Education in Namibia* (Windhoek).

Ministry of Education and Culture (1992c) *Discipline From Within* (Windhoek).

Ministry of Education and Culture (1993a) *Toward Education for All* (Windhoek: Gamsberg Macmillan).

Ministry of Education and Culture (1993b) *A Report on the Training of Trainers* (Windhoek).

Ministry of Education and Culture (1993c) *An Introduction to IGCSE and HGCSE* (Windhoek: University of Cambridge Local Examinations Syndicate/Ministry of Education and Culture).

Ministry of Education and Culture (1993d) *National Induction Seminar for Teacher Educators* (Windhoek).

Ministry of Education and Culture (1994) *Draft Syllabus: Primary Phase Social Studies Grade 4* (Windhoek).

Mkandawire, D. (1993) 'Teacher effectiveness in Namibian schools', in K. Prah (ed.) *Social Science Research Priorities for Namibia* (Windhoek: University of Namiba and the Council for the Development of Economic and Social Research in Africa).

Mmari, G. (1979) 'Teacher training in Tanzania', in H. Hinzen and V. H. Hundsdorfer (eds) *The Tanzanian Experience* (London: Evans Brothers).

Moll, I. (1995) 'For the sake of form: managing a rural South African school', unpublished paper.

Mosha, H. (1990) 'Twenty years after education for self-reliance: a critical review', *International Journal of Educational Development* 10(1): 59–68.

Moss, C. (1994) *Administering Education in Namibia: the Colonial Period to the Present* (Windhoek: Namibia Scientific Society).

Mwingira, A. C. (1968) Circular EDP P1/124/15 (Dar Es Salaam: Ministry of Education).

Nagel, T. (1992) *Quality Between Tradition and Modernity: Patterns of Communication and Cognition in Teacher education in Zimbabwe* (Pedagogisk Forskningsinstitut, University of Oslo).

Naidoo, J. (1996) 'Racial integration of public schools in South Africa', *Education Monitor* 7, 2.

Negash, T. (1987) *Italian Colonialism in Eritrea 1882–1941* (Stockholm: Almqvist and Wiskell International).

Ngugi wa Thiong'o (1992) 'From Bismark to Bush', *The South Supplement*, New Statesman and Society.

Nigerian Ministry of Information (1976) *Federal Republic of Nigeria Policy on Education* (Lagos: Government Printer).

Nigerian Secondary Schools Social Studies Project (1979) (Lagos: Heinemann).

Nyaggah, M. (1980) 'Apartheid and second-class education in South Africa', in A. Mugomba and M. Nyaggah (eds) *Independence Without Freedom* (Santa Barbara: ABC-Clio).

Nyerere, J. (1967) *Education for Self Reliance* (Dar Es Salaam: Government Printer).

O'Brien, D. (1972) 'Modernisation, order and the erosion of a democratic ideal: American political science 1960–1970', *Journal of Development Studies* 8: 351–78.

O'Callaghan, M. (1977) *Namibia: the Effects of Apartheid on Culture and Education* (Paris: UNESCO).

Obebe, B. (1980) Social Studies in Nigerian Schools For What? In Nigerian Educational Research Council Social Studies: Teaching Issues and Problems. Ethiope Publishing Corporation, Benin City.

Ochieng-Moya, L. A. (1985) *A Study of the Teaching of Social Studies in Selected Primary Schools in Kisumu and Siaya Districts*. M.Ed. dissertation. University of Nairobi.

ODA (1994) *Aid To Education in 1993 and Beyond* (London: ODA).

Odada, M. (1988) The State of Social Studies in Uganda. Paper submitted to the Executive Director, ASSP, Nairobi.

Ogula, A. P. H. (1985) A Study of Parents, Teachers and Pupils Attitudes Towards the Social Studies Curriculum and Relation to Pupil Achievement. Draft Research Report, Nairobi.

Oguntosin, B. (1985) Trends, Needs and Priorities in Social Studies Education in Nigeria. Report of the Seminar of the Co-ordinating Committee of ASSP, Nairobi.

Oroge, E. A. (1980) *The Dynamism of Social Studies as a Course of Study in the Developing Countries*. Nigerian Education Research Council, Lagos.

Osler, A. (1993a) 'Education for development and democracy in Kenya', *Educational Review* 45(2).

Osler, A. (1993b) 'Education for human rights and democracy in Ethiopia', *Human Rights Newsletters*.

Paden, J. (1973) *Religion and Political Culture in Kano* (Berkeley: University of California Press).

Paice, E. (1994) *Guide to Eritrea* (Chalfont St. Peter: Bradt).

Pampallis, J. (1988) 'The place of politics in people's education: the case of the Solomon Mahlangu Freedom College'. Paper presented at the National Political Education Workshop, Lusaka, Zambia, February 23–26.

Peil, M. (1976) *Nigerian Politics: The People's View* (London: Cassell).

Popkewitz, T. (ed.) (1987) *Critical Studies in Teacher Education* (Lewes: The Falmer Press).

Porter, A. (1979) 'The programme for political education: a guide for beginners', *Social Science Teacher* 8(3).

Pye, L. (1962) *Politics, Personality and Nation Building: Burma's Search for Identity* (New Haven: Yale University Press).

Pye, L. (1963) *Communication and Political Development* (Princeton: Princeton University Press).

Pye, L. (1966) *Aspects of Political Development* (Boston: Little, Brown).

Pye, L. and Verba, S. (eds) (1965) *Political Culture and Political Development* (Princeton: Princeton University Press).

Racing Ahead (1994) (Windhoek: Gamsberg Macmillan).

Rawnsley, A. (1990) 'The new wind of change', *The Guardian*, 11 Spetember 1990.

Rees, D. (1980) 'The Lesotho Model of Curriculum Development in Action'. Paper presented to ASSP.

Reid, K., Hopkins, D. and Holly, P. (1987) *Towards the Effective School* (Oxford: Blackwell).

Reimers, F. (1994) 'Education and structural adjustment in Latin America and sub-Saharan Africa', *International Journal of Educational Development* 14(2).

Rowell, P. (1995) 'Perspectives on pedagogy in teacher education: the case of Namibia', *International Journal of Educational Development* 15(1).

Rowell, P. and Prophet, R. (1990) 'Curriculum-in-action: the 'practical' dimension in Botswana classrooms', *International Journal of Educational Development* 10(1).

Royal Norwegian Ministry of Foreign Affairs (1993) *Support for Democratic Development* (Oslo: Ministry of Foreign Affairs).

Rugamba, R. (1990) *A Study of Teaching Methods Use in National Teachers' Colleges in Uganda*. Unpublished M.Ed. dissertation, University of Birmingham.

Rutter, M., Maughan, B., Mortimore, P. and Ouston, J. (1979) *Fifteen Thousand Hours* (London: Open Books).

Salia-Bao, K. (1991) *The Namibian Education System Under Colonialism* (Randburg: Hodder and Stoughton).

Salmon, C. and Woods, C. (1991) *Colleges of Education: Challenging the Cliche* (Durban: University of Natal Education Research Unit).

Sandbrook, R. (1976) 'The crisis in political development theory', *Journal of Development Studies* 12: 165–85.

Sanneh, L. (1975) 'The Islamic education of an African child', in G. Brown and M. Hiskett (eds) *Conflict and Harmony in Education in Tropical Africa* (London: George Allen and Unwin).

Saunders, M. (1982) 'Productive activity in the curriculum: changing the literate bias of secondary schools in Tanzania', *British Journal of Sociology of Education* 3(1): 39–55.

Schools Council (1981) *The Practical Curriculum* (London: Methuen).

Searle, C. (1981) *We're Building the New School!* (London: Zed Press).

Selassie, B. (1980) 'From British rule to federation and annexation', in B. Davidson, L. Cliffe and B. Selassie (eds) *Behind the War in Eritrea* (Nottingham: Spokesman).

Serote, P. (1992) 'Solomon Mahlangu Freedom College: a unique South African educational experience in Tanzania', *Transformation* 20.

Serpell, R. (1993) *The Significance of Schooling: Life Journeys in an African Society* (Cambridge: Cambridge University Press).

Shaeffer, S. (1990) 'Participatory approaches to teacher training', in V. Rust and P. Dalin (eds) *Teachers and Teaching in the Developing World* (New York: Garland).

Sherman, R. (1980) *Eritrea: The Unfinished Revolution* (New York: Praeger).

Shipman, M. (1971) *Education and Modernisation* (London: Faber & Faber).

Sierra Leone National Programme in Social Studies with Population (1984), Ministry of Education, Freetown.

Simbeye, E. K. (1985) A progress Report on Social Studies Education in Malawi. Report of the Seminar of the Co-ordinating Committee of ASSP, Nairobi.

Simuyu, V. (1988) 'The democratic myth in the African traditional societies', in W. Oyugi, E. Atieno Odhiambo, M. Chege and A. Gitonga *Democratic Theory and Practice in Africa* (London: James Currey).

Sithole, M. (1988) 'Zimbabwe: in search of a stable democracy', in L. Diamond, J. Linz and S. Lipset (eds) *Democracy in Developing Countries: Africa* (London: Adamantine Press).

Sivard, R. I. (1987) *World Military Expenditures* (Washington, DC: World Priorities).

Skinner, N. (1977) *Alhaji Mohmadu Koki* (Zaria: Ahmadu Bello University Press).

Sklar, R. (1986) 'Democracy in Africa', in M. Doro and N. Stultz (eds) *Governing in Black Africa* (London: African Publishing Company).

Smock, D. and Bentsi-Enchill, A. (1975) *The Search for National Integration in Africa* (New York: The Free Press).

Snyder, W. (1991) *Consultation on Change: Proceedings of the Etosha Conference* (Florida: Florida State University).

Stacey, B. (1978) Political Socialisation in Western Society (London: Edward Arnold).

SWAPO (1981) *To Be Born a Nation* (London: Zed Press).

SWAPO of Namibia Department of Education and Culture (1988) *Administrative Structure of SWAPO Education Centres* (Kwanza-Sul and Nyango).

Swaziland Primary School for Social Studies Series (1984) Ministry of Education, Mbabane.

Tabulawa, R. (1995) *Culture and Classroom Practice: A Socio-Cultural Analysis of Geography Classrooms in Botswana Secondary Schools' and Implications for Pedagogical Change.* Unpublished Ph.D. Thesis, University of Birmingham.

Tedesco, J. (1994) 'Knowledge versus values', *Educational Innovation* 78: 1–2.

Teklu, M. (1993) *Schools and Political Learning.* Unpublished B.Phil. Essay, University of Birmingham.

Tesfagiorgis, A. (1992) *A Painful Season and a Stubborn Hope* (Trenton, NJ: Red Sea Press).

Tesfamariam, T. (1993) *Democratic School Practice in Eritrea.* Unpublished Certificate of Education Essay, University of Birmingham.

The Gambia Primary Course, (1984) Ministry of Education, Youth, Sports and Culture, Banjul.

Tjitendero, M. (1982) *Policy Options for Basic Education.* Paper Presented to SWAPO Seminar on Education, Lusaka.

Tjitendero, M. (1984) *Education Policy for Independent Namibia* (Lusaka: United Nations Institute for Namibia).

Trafford, B. (1993) *Sharing Power in Schools: Raising Standards* (Ticknall: Education Now).

Trevaskis, G. (1960) *Eritrea: A Colony in Transition* (London: Oxford University Press).

Tunbridge, L. (1996) 'Moi's end game', *Focus on Africa,* January–March 1996.

Tuquoi, J-P. (1996) 'Chad under the shadow of the gun', *Guardian Weekly,* 14 April 1996.

Turner, J. (1990) *Education in Namibia* (Windhoek: Overseas Development Administration).

Udofoot, M. (1988) Training Social Studies Teachers for the Nigerian Schools. Paper submitted to the ASSP journal, Forum.

UNDP (1992) *Human Development Report* (New York: UNDP).

UNDP (1995) *Human Development Report* (Oxford: Oxford University Press).

UNDP (1996) *Human Development Report* (Oxford: Oxford University Press).

United Nations Institute for Namibia (1987) *Namibia: A Direct United Nations Responsibility* (Lusaka: UN).

United Nations Institute for Namibia (1989) *International Conference on Teacher Education for Namibia* (Lusaka: UN).

USAID (1993a) *Building Democracy: USAID's Strategy* (Washington: USAID).

USAID (1993b) *Namibia Basic Education Reform Program* (Windhoek: Creative Associates International).

User's Guide to the Education Code of Conduct (1993) (Windhoek: Ministry of Education and Culture).

Walker, J. (1980) 'The end of dialogue; Paulo Freire on politics and education', in R. Mackie (ed.) *Literacy and Revolution: the Pedagogy of Paulo Freire* (London: Pluto Press).

Walker, R. (1974) 'Classroom research: a view from SAFARI', in B. MacDonald et al. (eds) *SAFARI: Innovation, Evaluation, Research and the Problem of Control* (Norwich: CARE, University of East Anglia).

Ward, R. and Rustow, D. (1964) *Political Modernisation in Japan and Turkey* (Princeton: Princeton University Press).

Wasanga, C. M. (1987) *A Study of the Attitudes of Primary School Teachers Towards Social Studies in the Central Division of Machakos District.* M.Ed. dissertation, Kenyatta University, Nairobi.

Wentworth, B. (Undated) *Creating a Culture for Human Rights: A Summary History of the Culture of Care Development Trust* (Windhoek: Ministry of Education and Culture).

Wilson, A. (1991) *The Challenge Road: Women and the Eritrean Revolution* (London: Earthscan).

Wiseman, J. (1990) *Democracy in Black Africa: Survival and Revival* (New York: Paragon House).

Woldemichael, B. (1992) *Primary Education in Eritrea* Consultancy Report.

Wolpe, H. (1995) 'The struggle against apartheid education: towards people's education in South Africa', in V. McKay (ed.) *A Sociology of Educating* (Johannesburg: Lexicon).

World Bank (1988) *Education in Sub-Saharan Africa* (Washington, DC: World Bank).

World University Service (1994) *Education in Mozambique* (London).

Ya-Otto, J. (1982) *Battlefront Namibia* (London: Heinemann).

Zambia Ministry of Education (1977) *Teachers' Handbook for Social Studies* (Lusaka).

Zimba, R., Auala, R. and Scott, A. (1994) *Discipline Problems in Namibian Secondary Schools.* Paper presented to the Workshop of the Namibia Educational Management and Administration Society, Windhoek.

Index